ZIMBATÉ

A Path Toward A Truth

BY CAROLYN SNYDER

AND

LINDSEY GRIEVES, ARTIST

Copyright © 2012 Carolyn Snyder
All rights reserved.
ISBN: 1478288582
ISBN 13: 9781478288589
Library of Congress Control Number: 2012913500
CreateSpace, North Charleston, South Carolina

*I dedicate this book
with love and gratitude
to Enoch, Balzar, and
other Masters of the Universe.*

INTRODUCTION

Zimbaté, pronounced zim-ba-tay, is an ancient healing art given to us by Enoch and protected by the Ancient Great White Brotherhood. It has been used on Earth two previous times: firstly by the tribes started by Enoch, when Earth was first populated, and secondly by the Essenes, within their healing group called the Theraputi. The Great White Brotherhood removed Zimbaté from Earth. Both removals were due to the eventual misuse of its power. But we are in a time of great change, and the gift of Zimbaté is ours once again. The third time is now, for we are in great need, and many are ready to hold its powerful healing vibration in pure and clear intent.

My journey started in 1984 with Reiki. It was my constant life companion as well as my gift to share with others. In 1998, I joined a group in Oregon that was spiritually seeking growth and learning. This group eventually led to receiving the great gift of Zimbaté (the name it has now been given) from Enoch. It is a healing method and a life inspiration. It gently assists you on your life path and is the most remarkable healing modality I have encountered to date. Zimbaté has an exceptionally high vibration and is amazingly effective.

I feel drawn to share this gift and some of the insights I have gathered along the way. This book will take the mystery out of energy work and allow people to be comfortable with this often intangible and commanding field of ever-growing study. Spirituality meets science, student meets teacher. I believe that it is fear that holds us back; it prevents us from taking that leap of faith into the unknown. Fear comes from lack of knowledge or understanding. I hope this book eradicates fear through empowerment. This may be a new subject of interest for you. If so then I will help you navigate the language, background, and techniques involved in energy work. If you are like me and come from a background of spiritual learning but are seeking something more, then this book could be part of what you have been waiting for. Zimbaté is a unique opportunity; give it a chance, and see where it leads you.

Gratitude and love for each of you fills me. Thank you for picking up this book. I hope I am able to touch your life in a positive, active way. May your journey in life be sweet and full.

My heart is full of love for Enoch and Balzar. That they entrusted us with this exciting adventure is awe-inspiring.

- **Carolyn**

ZIMBATÉ

A Path toward a Truth

A system of touch, sounds, and vibration
For mind, body, and spirit,
Called Zimbaté (say zim-ba-tay).

Here, now, it is time for Zimbaté
For healing, positive change, and spiritual growth.

I invite you
To learn this powerful healing method.
It will complement your current practice:
Reiki, massage, other therapies.

To heal yourself,
To make positive changes in your life,
To know your path and progress toward your truth.

To heal others
And our planet Earth.

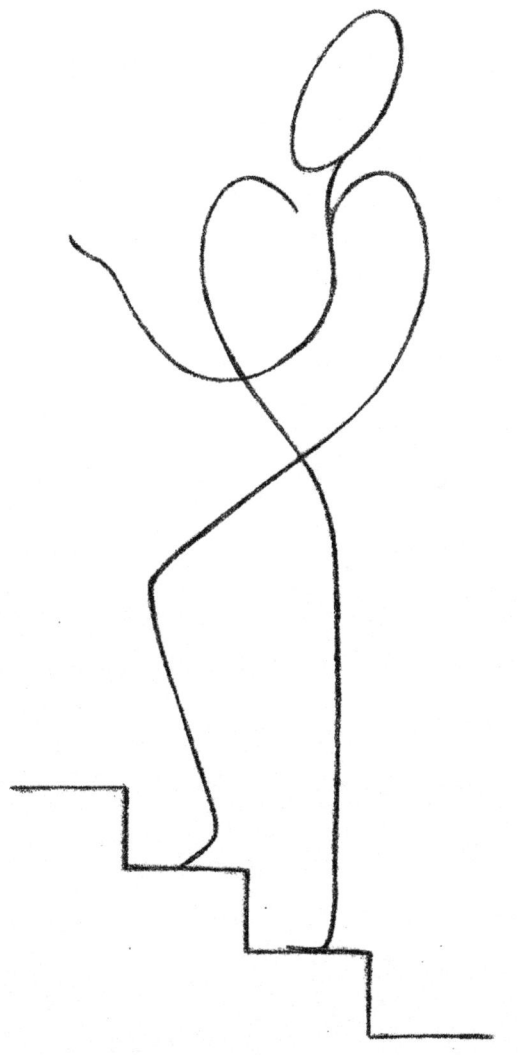

..... A Path to <u>a</u> Truth

ZIMBATÉ CREED

I hold Zimbaté wisdom with integrity.

I use Zimbaté energy with clear intent.

I am mindful of the responsibility entrusted in me.

I use Zimbaté with joy and generosity.

ACKNOWLEDGEMENTS

When Balzar first brought up the idea of a book, I panicked. I couldn't do that, no skill set, no knowledge. I stomped around, postponed even *thinking* about it, and did nothing. One night I had a 'dream'. In quite a stern voice I heard, "no pain, no gain." I was then flooded with the most beautiful love. I wrote the book.

Many people were influential in the journey that brought Zimbaté and me to the place where a book made sense. I give thanks every day to the people who make up my village.

My love and gratitude to Balzar, Enoch, and the Great White Brotherhood for bringing Zimbaté back at this time. I am honored and humbled to be a part of Zimbaté's return.

Steven Kirk, none of this would have been possible without you. Thank you.

Elizabeth Grande Doyle heard one of my first talks in Seattle. We met after the class, and she invited me to come to England to teach. Never in my wildest dreams could I have anticipated the journey she was instrumental in initiating. She has continued to graciously share her home. Thank you, Elizabeth.

My dear UK family, you bring great joy into my life. The friendships and support for me and for Zimbaté seem endless. You have been one of the great surprises of my life. Many of you I have journeyed with in past lives, and it is a rare pleasure that we meet again.

Simone and John Lamont-Black, you have been a blessing and a gift. Haven't we had fun! I appreciate your zest for life and your willingness to share adventures with me. You have given me tender memories Simone.

Rachel, you hold a very special place in my heart.

Lindsey Grieves, what a wonder you are! You are the living definition of the words "open heart." Thank you for the wonderful art you shared throughout the book. You are a creative and thoughtful artist. It has been amazing to watch you grow and expand as an artist and individual. You have much to share with the world, and it is going to be great fun to see that happen. She can be reached at lightsourceart.co.uk.

Claire Gillman, your article in *Kindred Spirit* helped launch Zimbaté in the UK. Your sage counsel about the book has been key in my continuing to write. Thank you for your friendship and warmth.

Jonathan Tarr and Siwan Quinn Bratton, I am still astonished at the synchronicity of our meeting and at how well our mutual intents fit. I am delighted with our connection and look forward to many years of working together. By the way, Jonathan has a magical way with the J Ray!

Lorraine Fardon a lovely human being and a brilliant word master! A great deal of the credit for any of the book's success is due to you. Not only did you help guide me, but also you are a wonderfully supportive friend. I have a grateful heart.

My family is wonderful. They support in me in whatever I do. I feel that they always have my back, and that gives me the freedom to take chances and explore the world in new ways. I love and appreciate each of you and your gifts.

- Carolyn

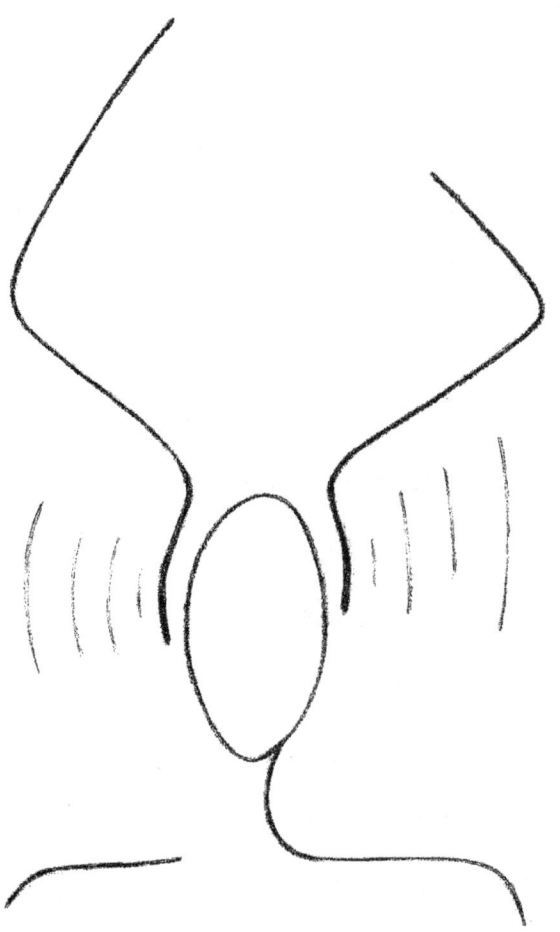

CHAPTER 1

MY BEGINNINGS

In 1984, I was at loose ends. I was a single mother of two wonderful girls, so I focused all my energy on raising them and earning a living. Personal fulfillment was not my first priority, but little did I know what wonderful things were about to unfold for me. At a meeting in downtown Seattle, a man approached me and asked if I was a healer. His question took me by surprise, slightly baffled me, but ignited a spark of interest. My strong response, coupled with his charm, persuaded me to meet him the next day for a walk around Green Lake in Seattle, Washington, (where I lived at the time). I'm eternally grateful that I did. He talked about working with energy, hands-on healing, and a class called Reiki. My intrigue grew, but what appealed to me most at that time was the fact that the class took place over a Friday night, all day Saturday, and all day Sunday. I had been looking for something to take my mind off a recent failed romance. I remember one of my first thoughts being, "I can fill a whole weekend!" The universe works in magical ways.

At this time in my life, spirituality was a non-event. I hadn't even considered what "spirituality" really meant to me. My first Reiki class prompted me to explore my beliefs, and my life quickly underwent a dramatic shift. The changes I felt fascinated me. I read everything I could get my hands on, and I took classes on a variety of related subjects. I immersed myself completely. I stayed up late and got up early, there was not enough time in the day for everything I felt compelled to learn. I walked around with "hot hands," testing the energy on everything: plants, animals, and the food I ate. I even managed to start a car battery using Reiki when I would have normally given up. The biggest surprise was that Reiki was reciprocal, so I was feeling more and more fulfilled with each new experience. Eventually, my body adjusted to the flow of energy, and my awareness of it became my new everyday norm.

In the western world, Reiki was still in its infancy. There were only twenty-two Reiki Masters, and Mrs. Hawayo Takata had initiated them all prior to her passing in 1980. To put this number into perspective, reports now indicate there are many hundreds of thousands of Reiki Masters worldwide. One of these initial twenty-two was Paul Mitchell; I was lucky enough to have him as my teacher.

Let me back-up a little. Dr. Mikao Usui founded Reiki, as we know it, in 1922 after he received enlightenment while meditating on a sacred spot around Mt. Kurama. In Japan, Reiki is a word used generically to describe various types of healing practice, so we should say that Usui Reiki is the specific and original practice Dr. Usui developed. He did so in line with what he learned upon Mt. Kurama along with his vast spiritual, psychological, and medical knowledge. Dr. Usui sought to expand the healing powers of Reiki, so he initiated the first Reiki Master, Dr. Churjiro Hayashi, in 1925.

Dr. Hayashi opened a Reiki clinic in Tokyo, and through his extensive knowledge of medicine and practical applications of such, he further developed the practice. In 1942, he treated a Japanese patient from Hawaii, Mrs. Takata, who was so impressed with the results of her treatments that she insisted he teach her. Dr. Hayashi was reluctant to have Reiki practiced outside of Japan, but eventually, satisfied with her clear intent, he shared his sacred knowledge. We can credit Mrs. Takata with bringing a streamlined, westernized version of Reiki to the western world. Reiki has now spread widely across the world and has evolved into many different forms. While most still have recognizable Usui origins, the variants are all subtly unique. This is not a criticism, for Reiki has been a great gift to the world, but looking back, I feel very blessed that the Reiki I received was in its purest and most undiluted form.

CHAPTER 2

THE NEXT STEP

Over the next fifteen years, I found Reiki to be the foundation, the anchor, of my healing practice. I took classes in other modalities, but I tended to tease out what didn't fit my individual journey and absorbed all that did. This is a part of the joy that practitioners can embrace and not restrained. What works for one may not work for another. We all have unique but equally valuable paths.

In the early days of my practice, I became aware of stepping outside of the accepted social flow of those close to me. Energy healing was not part of the social consciousness as it is today, and I felt very much that I was venturing into unchartered waters. While I was excited by the course that lay ahead, my family and friends struggled to understand what was happening in my life—the consensus fear being that I was going around the bend. Some were more able to accept these changes than others were, and despite the sadness of losing a special friend over our differences of beliefs, I continued to stay focused on my growth. This path was my true resonance and no turbulence had power enough to alter its course. Things continued with few major developments until 1992 when I found a like-minded group seeking personal growth, greater spiritual awareness, and a sense of community. I could never have foreseen how fundamentally my course would alter by my connection to this group.

I'm about to take you along on my journey, and wish you to remain open-minded and operate in a realm of faith and intuition. Our human existence is often caught up in the illusion of the shared experience that is "reality." To sometimes consciously break away from this restriction and suspend rigid shared belief systems, opens up a whole new, truer, more empathic sense of reality. We allow ourselves to explore the immense realms of possibility that set us free from our strictly human, secular selves.

Here goes—all you need to do now is sit back and listen, and we'll talk over the details later. I had previously been in the presence of channeled beings, and while I had found the experience immensely interesting, I had not felt any particular drive to explore this area further. This all changed when I met Balzar, at the group I just mentioned, in Klamath, Oregon.

Balzar is a being from the Ancient Mystical Great White Brotherhood who uses Steve Kirk's body to communicate with us. It is called channeling. Steve was a firefighter (captain) when, in 1991, he had an epiphany that brought him (literally and figuratively) to his knees. A being named Balzar had channeled through him, and he was soon to act as channel for other beings, including Enoch—you may have never heard these names before, but hold those thoughts and bear with me; I will tell you more about the Brotherhood in the following chapter. For now, let us go back to Steve. Steve was completely unaccustomed to this new arena of experience, and it took almost a full year for him to comprehend the commitment and changes that channeling would mean to his life. He made the decision to dedicate himself to being available at all times of day and night. Steve opened an herbal shop and offered counseling and classes. Steve is a full-body channel, which means that when Balzar is "in," he has full control over Steve's body; he talks, walks, and has a different "look" and energy from Steve.

Whenever Balzar was "in the body," it meant that Steve was "out." Steve would "return" and have no idea of what had transpired during that time. This may sound fearful to some, but similar to being under hypnosis, the subconscious remains active, so nothing could be done against Steve's will. He always has free will. As Steve's body became more accustomed to the exchange, Balzar would be with us for greater periods of time, sometimes upward of twelve hours on a given day. Steve's selfless willingness to channel seems all the more remarkable when we consider the toll it must have taken on his body and the immense sacrifice of his own awareness of life's experiences. But Steve never once complained about his calling, and to this day, he remains very humble about his significant contribution. Without Steve, we would not have the gift of Balzar, Enoch, and their great teachings. I have great admiration and gratitude for your contribution Steve; thank you.

Now, back to the journey. Balzar's classes were different from my previous experiences: they were challenging and provoking. Balzar did not simply provide information or offer insights. He presented situations on topics that required great effort and honesty on our part to explore. We were encouraged to appreciate our *individual* truths, which facilitated unique and seemingly tailor-made personal growth. In one early class, Balzar offered to spend a few minutes with each of us privately. I was a tad nervous and didn't know what I wanted to talk about; I just knew I wanted this to *count*! We sat down at a small table on the patio, and out of the blue, without prior thought, I asked the question, "How are we going to work together?" I was appalled, and to this day, I have no idea where that question came from. Balzar, in his infinite patience, politely replied that we would talk about our work together at a later date. In case you haven't guessed already, this book is one result of my work with Balzar, but that day was not the right time for its discussion. I learned that all that is right and true would be granted its time, at the right time.

During one of my favorite weekends, we studied the book *Nine Faces of Christ: Quest of the True Initiate* by Eugene E. Whitworth. Balzar assigned each of us a section of the book to study and asked us to present it back to the group after an hour, with our interpretation of the esoteric meanings. As with any powerful spiritual text, it had a compelling and easily accessible surface story, but woven beneath the surface was a complex web of deeper meaning. We learned to look beyond the words to find the greater knowledge, often seemingly hidden. These classes were not ones we could bluff our way through; we really had to know our stuff. This was a valuable lesson in itself. Dedication grants great rewards, and the knowledge we received as reward was highly prized indeed.

Not everything was classroom style; we got to enjoy some great adventures! A special event for our group was our regular pilgrimage to Mount Shasta in California. Some years were trickier than others due to snowfall and snowmelt, and sometimes we made it to the peak, others not. It never mattered. The lessons we were to learn appeared to fit seamlessly into the apparently aimless wanders in "Mr. B's" presence (the apparent aimlessness of the wanderings was only so to us; I have no doubt Balzar knew exactly the path that lay ahead). On one occasion we wandered across a small bubbling spring, the headwaters of the Sacramento River. The water was very sweet. We followed that infant stream for a time, found a lovely meadow, and listened to Balzar recounting stories about the mountain. It was casual and easy that day, but the personal insights remained as poignant as some of the more challenging days were. This is another important lesson. Learning is multilayered; lessons reside in everything, and knowledge blooms equally from challenging roots as it does from simple ones—we just need to be open to receiving it. Mount Shasta is indeed a blissful place. In her presence I felt nurtured, and I would suggest to others that they visit Mount Shasta to revel in her grace.

My lessons under Balzar's guidance continued until around 2003 when we were initiated into the healing energy that is called Zimbaté by Enoch. Balzar's intent in coming to us and teaching us was to bring it back to the world. Zimbaté is a beautiful, pure, and intense healing energy that we need now, more than ever, in these turbulent times. At the time of this writing, Balzar is still accessible, but he is mostly working with those of us who are doing Zimbaté. I will talk more about Zimbaté later in this book, but for now, I must fulfill my earlier promise to tell you about the Brotherhood…

.....Wisdom

CHAPTER 3

A MESSAGE FROM BALZAR

THE ANCIENT MYSTICAL GREAT WHITE BROTHERHOOD AND BALZAR

The Ancient Mystical Great White Brotherhood exists in the fifth dimension and is one of the Brotherhoods we hear about most often. You may have heard the Brotherhoods mentioned in relation to the Sumerians who lived around 6000 BC as well as in current day discussions around the evolution of collective perception. The Brotherhood was formed to preserve certain spiritual teachings that humankind would find useful in facilitating continued evolution and in reaching our full potential. The Brotherhood is a collective of beings that guide, instruct, and protect in close relation to Mother Earth. We could view them as Earth's spiritual guardians. The "white" of the Brotherhood refers to the highest form of thinking—the encompassing of all and everything, just as all the colors of the rainbow are manifest in white light.

Balzar is part of one of the Brotherhood who is compelled, through his remarkable love and belief in humankind, to guide and instruct those of us who have open hearts and are willing to learn. I know we try his patience, but his staying power is strong. Balzar is at once a master trickster and weaver of words, but he teaches with simplicity and humor. In our sessions his presentation was informal, and participation from the group was expected. He didn't sit on a stage and lecture and he did not have an entourage—it was just Balzar and his students.Balzar's teachings are under the direction of the Brotherhood. I would like to share with you what he wrote and shared with me some years ago. I think it answers many questions you may have at this point:

> Yours is a world of *arrogance* and *competition,* and you are destroying the planet you call home. Not only is humanity suffering but so are the plants and animals that share this planet. It is true that you have been granted *free will* by the Creator, but most of you are exercising it without taking personal responsibility for your actions. Your once "Garden of Eden" has been literally turned into a garbage heap.
>
> I come from a dimension where we do not experience competition because we have come to the understanding that we are all part of the whole. We may disagree because we still have free will, but we have learned to settle our differences while continuing to remain in a state of harmony and balance.
>
> It requires great patience for us to interact with humanity. Often your actions are irrational and irresponsible. Even your perception of the information and ideas we present to you varies greatly from individual to individual. Let me emphasize that all information presented by a member of the Ancient Mystical White

Brotherhood contains the same content, but it will vary in working and presentation.

My ultimate purpose for being here and interacting with each of you is to help you grow and evolve by aligning your body, mind, and spirit. Eventually this will enable you to reach the enlightened state of being at one with God. My teachings are universal, and I teach under the direction of the Ancient Mystical Great White Brotherhood. I choose to teach with humor and use simple language. I am not here to impress you, but I am here to *make an impression on you*.

Many channels and much channeled information are available on your planet at this time. To accelerate your spiritual growth, all you have to do is listen with an open heart and open mind to the information available to you. I am here to give you guidance and reveal how best to live your life. How you live your life is your choice. I am here to help you learn to take personal responsibility for your actions. Many times my methods of teaching involve enhancing circumstances at the request of your soul to accelerate your personal growth. These lessons are never easy because *you* do the action to gain the wisdom. Some of you are able to learn by going through the first circumstance and gain the wisdom, but others may have to repeat the circumstances many times before gaining the wisdom. The soul only presents lessons or experiences to promote the strength of an individual, as does self-examination. Therefore, I use these methods frequently and oftentimes push you beyond your perceived limitations.

I also use, and will continue to use, comparative illusions because they make you think before you make a choice or decision. This is quite different from a lie. Lies do not benefit you in any way. They promote external power and are deliberately misleading. Simply put, comparative illusions provide you with choices... choices to move through your fears. *I will never tell you anything that will not serve you.*

I present you with suggested and required reading as a basis or entry point into the concepts I am here to clarify. This method is time effective, but most importantly, it requires diligence on your behalf. Spiritual growth comes from personal effort. You can only really own what you have by working to learn and understand. Discernment is also an important attribute you must learn. It requires that you learn to trust your intuition when presented with conflicting information. Discernment does not mean that you believe everything you hear or read. Only you know what is true for you, and your truth will evolve as you evolve.

Commitments are easily made but difficult to keep. All of you have been presented with situations that require personal commitments of varying degrees. All require perseverance to complete. How they are handled speaks much of your dependability and character. Eventually, you must all learn to walk your talk, and that takes tremendous courage.

True service to all of God's creations is done through love and humility. Recognition of services provided is born of ego. The unselfish act of small kindnesses you extend to others is what matters. Mastership is not attainable until you are able to effect a positive change in others by example.

You must all develop the faith to go "within" for your answers. All of the knowledge and wisdom that you will ever need lies within you. An empowered individual sees the perfection of each situation. And each experience is for the evolution of the soul and the maturation of the personality...the perfection of God in the imperfection of man.

I honor and love each and every one of you. Your spiritual journey is what you make it. I suggest you relax and learn to enjoy life. Then, when you encounter difficulties and obstacles (as you all must) resolve them as quickly and efficiently as possible. Allow yourself to experience what it is to learn, step by step, the freedom that comes from being unattached to the outcome. Live in the trust that when the timing is appropriate, the pieces will fall into place, and you will see the clarity that is the perception of wisdom. Perceive and understand the illusion in which you live in the third dimension, and let it play out to its conclusion. Clarity is simply the ability to see the soul in action in the physical world.

With my deepest Gratitude and Love.

Namaste,

Balzar

.... Enoch

CHAPTER 4

A SHORT HISTORY OF ZIMBATÉ

This is the third time that Zimbaté energy has been on our planet Earth. Four million years ago, there was the Land of Enoch. This was before the time of Atlantis. It was located near what we now call Mexico. Enoch placed seven tribes on earth and brought many light bodies to assist them. These tribes were made of human man; they had density. Beings in other dimensions do not have weight or bulk, i.e. density to their person. It is only on Earth that we have solidity. These celestial beings or light bodies brought celestial energy (what we now call Zimbaté) to use and share with humankind. Over time, some of the light bodies became infatuated with the possibilities they saw on Earth—things like power and the idea of "more." They discovered separation from their source, God. They developed greed, jealousy, and other human traits. The land of Enoch eventually sank into the sea. Consequently, the celestial energy was also lost.

Other light bodies from this period had remained pure in their intent and motives. They moved to the valley of Airyana, somewhere between two rivers whose names we now know as the Tigris and Euphrates. Their homeland was called the Valley of the Heart. They eventually became physical and developed a way of life that embraced moral teachings and the art of healing. They were called the Watchers. In time, these 200 Sumerians became part what we now call the Ancient Mystical Great White Brotherhood.

The second appearance of Zimbaté on Earth was with the Essene culture based in Qumran. The original group of Essenes was the greatest gathering of Ascended Masters ever assembled on Earth. They were from the Ancient Mystical Great White Brotherhood and the Galactic realm.

The Essenes had a sect called the Theraputi. They were the ones who taught and shared their healing technique. The Theraputi used their hands in sharing the energy and always asked for the presence of their guides while healing. Because the energy had such power, some who learned from the Theraputi abused the privilege of the energy. The students tried to use the energy to gain much through the exploitation of power. When the abuse continued, the ability to transfer the energy to another was removed by the White Brotherhood. After a period of time, it was seen that the integrity of healing was continually abused, so the energy was completely removed by the celestial counterparts. This meant that human man could no longer transfer healing energy to others.

Today, Enoch and Balzar are returning this gift of Celestial Energy to us. They are calling it Zimbaté. People often ask, "Why us, and why now?" The answer Enoch and Balzar give is simple. There are people today who are ready to bring it to life again. They have proper intent and motive. Also, the earth is in need of our love and healing. Zimbaté is such a great gift to the world, but a gift holds a precious responsibility. If you are reading this book, I trust there is something in this for you. How will you respond? Zimbaté will draw some of you out, and you will seek it. Others might not be ready and have no place in their lives for Zimbaté. There is no right or wrong. There is no judgment.

Of course there is more to this story. Balzar would suggest that you do some research of your own. Information has greater value and impact when you impart effort and use your own energy to uncover it. May I suggest you study the Essenes? Enoch? These subjects can lead you to many more topics of value and interest.

CHAPTER 5

PERSONAL LESSONS

In chapter 3 Balzar talked about his methods of teaching. He mentioned enhancing circumstances, of which he is a master. To give you a better idea of what an enhanced circumstance is and how it can change your perceptions (and life), here is an example from my own experience.

An issue for me in this lifetime is using my backbone when dealing with people and situations. I have a backbone, I just didn't use it often enough! Standing up for and supporting myself has not been my greatest strength. This weakness has led to downfalls in the past and is a large part of my history I have needed to tackle. I'm not so great with conflict either. Because these were both areas of myself I needed to address, Balzar enhanced circumstances around me that called for me to be strong. I "got it" some of the time, although often enough I did the avoidance dance. Balzar's hints got firmer. I danced harder. It was miserable for me, and you can probably imagine the scene. Everything in life seemed increasingly to push my buttons. Nothing I was doing seemed to be working, and I certainly wasn't getting what I wanted! That is an example of enhanced circumstances—when the individual experiences that you need to face, in order to spiritually evolve, get more intense so you can't easily ignore them anymore.

During one class Balzar had me stand in front of the group while he told me to get my act together. I needed either to make adjustments or move on. He needed committed people, and I needed to make a decision. That was one scary moment in time. However, it became a turning point for me. I had a clear and firm look at the fear I was continuing to nurture. Was I willing to let go of the fear? Was I committed to my personal growth? Was I strong enough to implement the changes if I made the commitment? How would I do it? The questions kept coming thick and fast, alongside the excuses.

I spent some time alone, away from the group. It was make or break time. Did I want to stay in the group? It was obvious that to continue studying with Balzar I needed to fully commit to answering all the questions and overcoming the excuses. This was not a free ride. Balzar was with us to make a difference in our lives; if I didn't want to make positive changes, it would be best if I found something else to do. At one point that afternoon, I made the full commitment to change. I had made the leap and was now on an uncertain journey.

Later that same afternoon, I stood in front of the group and told Balzar that I was really tired of the fear I generated when faced with conflict, real or imagined. I wanted to change, and I wanted to stay in the group. I wanted to work hard to recognize situations when they arose for the fear they harbored and face up to them squarely. What was remarkable for me is that my statement became, as I said it, a pledge, and one that truly came from my heart. I felt liberated as I said the words. I felt strong, capable, and *free*!

As time progressed, my previous fears began to melt away. Conflicts didn't develop as they had in the past, and solutions came more easily. I learned one of my greatest lessons: when the issue is resolved within yourself, the universe no longer needs to present you with challenging (and often unpleasant) enhanced circumstances. Dealing with issues is far preferable to the suffering of avoidance. I began to recognize and understand situations that represented my own brand of patterning before they became an issue. I was able to see the misery and grief I created for myself by running from situations that previously would have filled me with worry and self-doubt. It is so much easier to deal with circumstances when they occur. The alternative is allowing them to become painful and color your whole being, and there is no fun in that! Sure, we can hope they go away, and they often appear to, but if we are committed to personal growth then confront them we must, and sooner is always better than later. Truthfully, being human, I still show occasional weakness in standing up to a situation. It is rare, and I recognize it for what it is and try to be gentle and forgiving with myself. But the fear I previously felt is no longer a part of the operational me.

.... Internal power

FACING YOUR FEARS

Facing your fears can call for immense personal strength, but it's often not nearly as terrifying as you might think. Somehow, we seem to associate our human issues with failure and fear it will be painful to acknowledge our deficiencies, as we view them. I wonder how we have learned that fears are bad; we are ever so reluctant to even talk about them. I know that in the past, talking about my fears, even with myself, was something I found daunting.

However, the rewards for dealing with fears and issues are tremendous. Life is fuller, brighter, and so satisfying. Have you ever put off paying your bills for fear of not having enough money and feeling overwhelmed by what bills are due? It sits somewhere in your head and won't leave. It starts to make you anxious, but you keep putting it off—the fear gets bigger, you lose sleep, and so the monthly pattern continues. Think of it this way: if you wait until the tenth or twelfth of the month to pay your bills, you have taken some of the joy out of your life for a quarter of the month. Rather wasteful, don't you think? *Man up! Get the bills out, do what you need to do to put the finances in order, and then revel in how good you feel!* Life should feel good; why rob your life of joy through inaction? Taking positive actions will assist you in overcoming your blocks. You will feel lighter, freer, and more in control. Doing nothing will ensure those blocks remain, and it will leave you feeling anxious, cranky, and fearful. It's a no-brainer when you look at each situation from that perspective.

Often, our current fears have evolved from a situation that we created to protect ourselves. Fear is a healthy, normal aspect of life that helps keep us safe, but over time, fears can gain power and exert control over more than the situation that created it. When you feel that pull to the negative side, stay present, do Zimbaté, or simply ask for assistance in determining the appropriate and meaningful course of action. Pay attention, and watch for the signposts that will help you make healthy decisions and changes.

If your house, car, or workspace is messy, does it leave you edgy? Tackle it, and life will smooth right out. I know messiness can seem a relatively small thing, but a cluttered living space can represent or exacerbate a disordered mental or emotional state. We all need to be a bit messy sometimes, but when it drives you up a wall, that's when it demands your attention. Sometimes it takes time and patience to find out what is unsettling us. What is getting in the way of you being centered, peaceful, and at ease in your world? Be honest. Take a good look. Any action, activity, or relationship that is not centered and bringing you satisfaction could be a problem area. You might find that any action or thought in a positive direction will start the ball rolling to a healthier outlook. The speed at which it does when you are willing might pleasantly surprise you. Too simplistic to work? No, the real solutions are generally simple and clear, it is our humanness that muddies the water and makes life hard.

no mind...
no mind...
no mind...

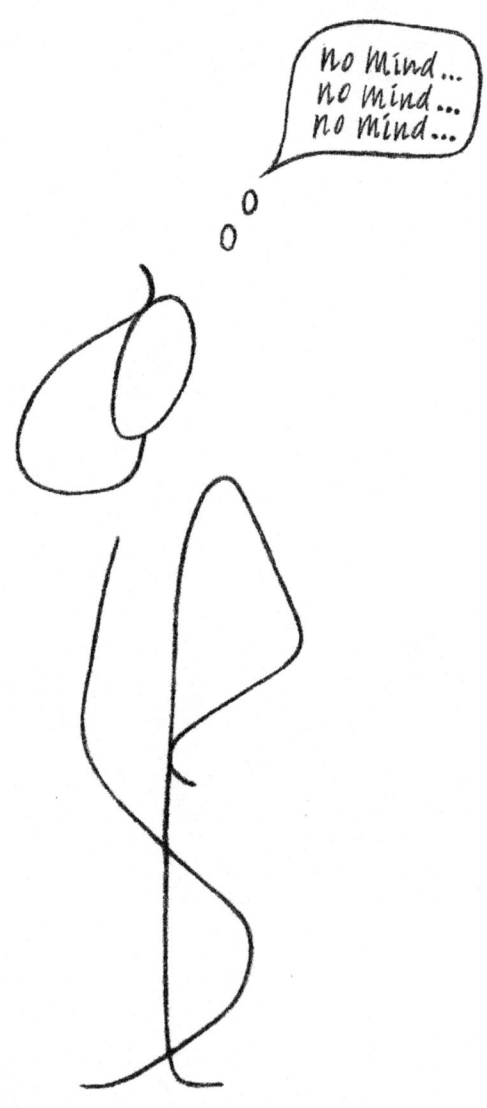

.....its none of my business
what people think of me!

CHAPTER 6

WORKING WITH BALZAR

Classes, outings, and gatherings with Balzar continued through the years. Subjects ranged from studying the beginnings of major religions to esoteric learnings. We enjoyed simple everyday activities, and each and every one had learnings attached. Balzar's teachings were always intriguing and often had a twist. One memorable teaching came from Balzar sending us all to a Wal-Mart to interact with customers. He told us to engage at least four customers in conversations. I was with my daughter, and we had a few giggles and lots of fun. Some people wouldn't engage, while others were a total surprise. We had a couple of truly meaningful conversations with people I would not normally have approached. I know that I often made snap judgments based on appearance, age, body language, and even a person's expression. Some people in the class had amazing experiences that led them to "aha" moments. Our lesson? Don't judge—people can be a great revelation, and everyone has value. It was humbling to discover what we so often miss by being dismissive or presumptuous.

That evening in the Wal-Mart, Balzar enhanced our circumstances so we would have a full experience based on our individual needs. Everybody's experiences were consequently different. Balzar always utilized various methods depending on the particular teaching. He *never* manipulated us or forcibly changed our life path, the Great White Brotherhood forbids this. Balzar would instead place us in situations that encouraged us to challenge our view of the world and our own place within it. He empowered us to see past the *status quo*, to make new and better individual choices. If personal growth stemmed from an experience then that was great in Balzar's eyes, but if we didn't change, that was good too. There was no judgment, no pressure; he simply granted opportunities for change and then continued to love us regardless. Balzar showed us unconditional love. As the years went on, I began to realize that nothing we had experienced in the classes was without purpose. He orchestrated our time together from the first minute to the last.

The longer I spent in Balzar's presence, the better I was able to understand the complexity of his work with us. But some of this understanding came in hindsight, as greater understanding often does. We cannot foresee circumstances, and unique interpretations are inherent within our individuality and, therefore, difficult to override. We too often jump to conclusions based on our most recent or most prominent experiences. For example, on my last trip to England, Balzar suggested I seek an interaction with a fellow flyer. I ended up having a delightful time discussing healing and pro-athletics with a couple that lived in the town I was flying into. That conversation enhanced my ideas regarding an article I had been asked to write, and, as a consequence, my article was better because I was able to present a broader point of view. I was grateful to Balzar for encouraging me to open up to the possibility of that enlightening interaction.

Balzar suggested to me that another "occurrence" would take place on my return plane journey. Based on my recent pleasant experience, my mind went to that easy place of acceptance, and I was looking forward to another great conversation. No such luck. The occurrence turned out to involve two medical emergencies on board, one of which resulted in the stricken passenger dying. I quickly realized I had closed myself off to any possible occurrence other than a pleasant one because of the expectations and prior judgments that had clouded my awareness. Balzar had shown me the misguided power of assumptions.

CHAPTER 7

RESPOND OR REACT?

Assumptions are one pitfall, but reactions can present even greater obstacles to our growth and understanding. Have you ever wondered at the variety of your interactions with other people? Why are some enjoyable and easy, while others are irritating and difficult? What triggers are at work? One reason may be the "response and react" action. Let me explain. When we have a *reaction* to a person, situation, or experience, it is an instant feeling, and it is generally a negative one. Often it will be strong and sure; there is no doubt in your mind that you do not like what is going on or do not like the person who triggered the feeling. That person triggered a reaction before you were even consciously aware of it. This unconscious kind of behavior can highlight weak areas of your personality. For example, the "offending" person may actually be *mirroring your own behavior.* It may sound surprising, but a basic in psychological thought is that we often dislike in others what we dislike in ourselves. Behaviors in others that we unconsciously recognize as our own weaknesses or failures trigger strong and immediate emotional reactions. Such reactions can be physical in nature and can be stronger and more instantaneous than the thought process. We might

33

speak harshly or cruelly, certainly judgmentally. We simply cannot stand that behavior *in them.* You certainly don't want that person in your life; better to dismiss them now than put up with all the negative feelings they bring up in you. Right?

Here is a dynamic way to look at such a situation. What if that person contracted with you (before you were born) to help you see yourself as you really are and help you develop your personal knowledge? (Play along here!) When that person generates such a charged reaction, it is as if a mirror is being held up to your inner self, and the parts of yourself you maybe need to change are reflecting glaringly back at you. Whenever I react to a person or situation in such a way as I have described, I know there is something there that I need to address in my own life. Life presents us with many and varied opportunities in this field. Some we get immediately, and some we are not yet ready to recognize. Several years ago, a mutual friend wanted Theresa and I to meet, as she was sure we'd love each other as much as she loved each of us. Over lunch, Theresa and I sniped and snapped at one another, which resulted in an awkward time for all. I was very glad when it was over. I certainly felt I didn't like her much. Our mutual friend was shocked at our display of childish behavior and bad manners. After some time had passed, I realized that we had both been mirroring for each other. I took a hard look at my reactions and could see, in myself, what I thought I did not like in Theresa. I started to pay attention to my reactions to others I encountered, and I began to change my patterns. I brought Zimbaté energy in to assist me, and I believe that it made the process faster and easier.

Respond or React?

A couple of years later, Theresa called and asked for my help in dealing with her breast cancer. Her call greatly surprised me, and I waited with interest for her first appointment. It was like meeting a different person! There was no animosity or negative reaction. It was a breath of fresh air. We had both made changes and had grown. We have since enjoyed a successful and fulfilling professional and personal relationship. Today we have a special bond, and I think she is remarkable woman. We have laughed about that first lunch and given thanks for our growth.

So now, let's talk about responding versus reacting. When I can see an event or relationship clearly, calmly, and without that punch of negative emotional involvement, the result can be a response rather than a reaction. A response is proactive rather than reactive; it has the feeling of measured consideration. There is a distance, a removal of ego involvement that is freeing. When you reach the point where you can respond to a situation, rather than react, you have taken thoughtful control of your participation; you are present rather than letting the subconscious take control. There is no emotional trauma, no pain body involved (refer to the works of Eckhart Tolle for great exploration of personal pain bodies and how they cloud judgment), and you can think clearly and measure your answers and actions against your truer self. There is no instant feeling (usually negative). Instead, you feel objective and removed and can see the situation clearly rather than through a haze of emotion.

When a situation suggests a problem that I might want to address within myself, it can be a hard idea to swallow. However, I know that a healthy way to see difficult lessons is to treat them as opportunities for personal freedom and growth. Positive change can be exhilarating. If you have a "button pusher" in your life (and don't we all?), look for mirroring, and see how fast you can solve the puzzle of where that button is wired to within you. Real freedom is not having as many buttons to push. It is exhilarating to encounter someone after a period of time and realize they are unable to affect you as they did in the past; you have changed and no longer need that negative reaction to help in your growth.

One of the greatest benefits of personal growth is your ability to meet each day with balance and calm. Most of our stress is people related, so when you reduce the number of times a day you react to others, you reduce your stress and increase your vitality. Once you have mastered the knack of catching your "mirrors" you will find they have a recognizable pattern, and once you have mastered the pattern, well, it becomes easier and easier! Zimbaté can assist many lessons and life situations. Just bring Zimbaté in to your body (you are taught how in class) when you are in the middle of your "stuff" and ask for help. It really is that simple.

.....the gift of Zimbate

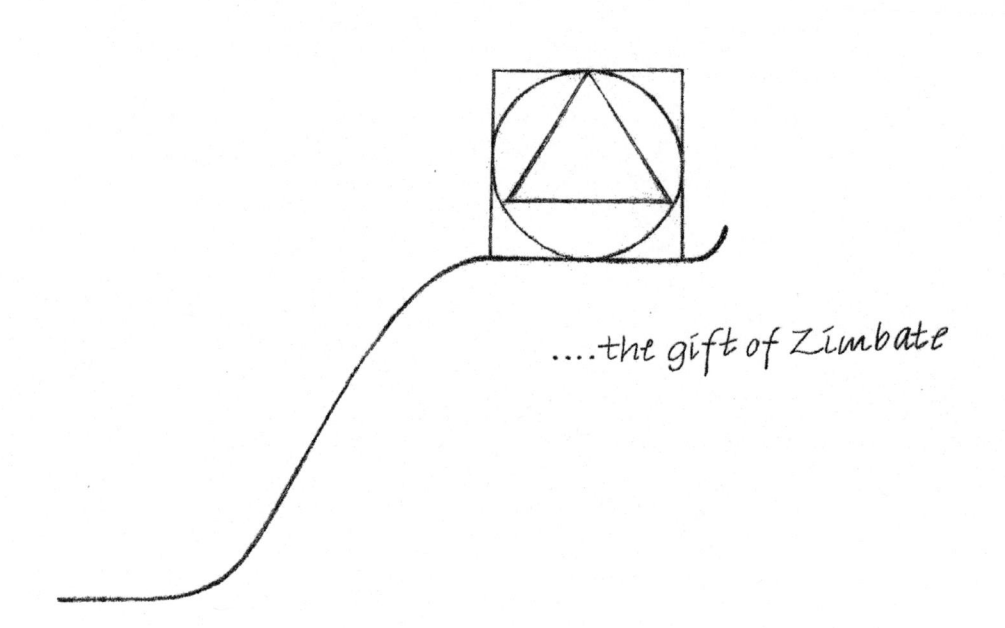

CHAPTER 8

MY INTRODUCTION TO ZIMBATÉ

In the early summer of 2003, after ten years of learning, inspiration, and growth, Balzar asked five of our group to come to Steve's home for a weekend. This was the first time there were no topic details or plan of action for the weekend. It turned out to be a life-changing weekend, although I certainly didn't realize it at the time.

Although Balzar was our primary channel, others came in from time to time. One such person was Enoch, the patriarch of our planet Earth. Enoch is different from Balzar; he is soft-spoken, quiet, and carries himself with dignity. There is a reserve about him that commands full attention and respect. He has an aura of calm, wisdom, and knowledge.

On that Saturday, Enoch was channeled through Steve, and he talked about a healing technique called Zimbaté. He shared with us the history, the techniques, and how we could use Zimbaté to help others as well as for our own fulfillment. Enoch then initiated each of us so we would have the ability to share Zimbaté; in addition, we were also given the gift to teach, and, thereby, to pass on this sacred knowledge to others.

Over the weekend we were provided with references to earlier classes and workshops to better aid our comprehension. It seemed that Enoch gave us a lot of information in no particular order, and by the end of the first day, I had an impression of jumbled and out-of-sequence knowledge. The next day, Sunday, when we practiced with each other, I did not have any special sense of the Zimbaté energy or its effectiveness. However, I did find the energy comfortable and easy to use. On Sunday night, on my way home, I felt a little confused and uncertain about Zimbaté. In truth, it didn't seem like a big deal, and I wasn't sure how it would fit with Reiki.

For the next week or so, I reflected on all the facts I had about Zimbaté. I mulled over what I should do, and I called a friend to ask if she would be willing to try out a new technique I had just learned. She graciously said she would be my guinea pig. We had previously experienced several Reiki sessions together, and she had taken my Reiki classes. I felt that her solid knowledge of Reiki and energy work was good, so I reasoned that it would be a proper setting for a trial run of Zimbaté.

For those of you acquainted with Reiki you know that a session generally lasts about an hour. I worked on my friend with my Zimbaté skills, and the session took about fifteen minutes, not the hour or so we had expected. I could not find anything else in her body that wanted work. She said she felt "done." After a few minutes, I checked her using Reiki and was unable to find any additional needs or areas that called for further work. I felt a little out of balance. I found myself apologizing because the session had taken no time at all. Did she feel cleared and comfortable? I asked her for feedback. She told me that she was thrilled, that she felt great, and that she could not have been more pleased that it took so little time to feel this good.

My next experience with Zimbaté was about a week later when I asked a very special client if I could share this new modality with her. Elise had battled breast cancer for the previous three years, and the cancer had spread to her lungs and brain. She had endured chemotherapy, radiation, surgery, the whole nine yards. When I started to work with her, she asked me to focus on helping her reduce pain and enabling her to enjoy the best possible quality of life. She was active in her process and was wonderfully spiritually aware. Working with her was a joy. That afternoon she was having trouble breathing. She had a new tumor on her right lung and asked if we could focus on that area of her body. After about five minutes, I started to sweat, as in roll-down-my-face sweat—none of that ladylike glow for me! I have since found that when the energy is powerful, I really start to sweat. Elise and I looked at each other, and we both knew that something was happening. After a few minutes, the energy began to fade. Elise took a deep breath; she found she could breathe more deeply than before. She said, "The tumor has gone; I can breathe." I was stunned by her response and by what we had both just felt. A later X-ray showed that the tumor had indeed shrunk.

Having worked with Elise over an extended period of time, this was a wholly different session than either of us had previously experienced. I was physically and emotionally shaky when Elise and her mom left. I felt I had experienced something incredible and was astounded on several levels. Zimbaté was fast, effective, and focused but at the same time gentle. What did I have here? I needed to regroup. Zimbaté was certainly more than another type of Reiki or other hands-on healing energy work. I was thrilled and full of wonder, but also a little overwhelmed. This was bigger and different from anything I had felt during the twenty-five years of my healing practice. I needed to share this, but how? My questions became endless.

I called Steve and asked to speak with Balzar. Balzar and I talked for some time about my response to the session with Elise and about Zimbaté in general. By the end of our conversation, I had agreed to take all the information given to us and format it into a manual for teachers and students. That felt like an achievable goal and a step in the right direction toward sharing this amazing energy. One step at a time.

It took me several months to complete my own personal integration and make sense of all the crazy notes I had taken over the years. It was interesting to see that, for a number of years, Balzar had been giving us small pieces of Zimbaté; we just didn't know it at the time. I wrote and rewrote. I bugged Balzar over details. I completed draft after draft and found that I was able to make the information simpler and simpler. Once I had it organized, I found that there was actually very little to memorize and learn. Zimbaté was *intuitive*. As I developed my relationship with Zimbaté, I realized that it felt like pure *God Intent*. It felt clean and clear. It did not have any of the human tricks or rituals that I had often wondered about in the past with other modalities.

Finally, in the fall of 2003, I held a trial class. I had asked several of my friends who had taken Reiki classes from me, and who were knowledgeable about energy systems, to take that class. This was a leap of faith for me, as I certainly didn't want to fail in front of them. The class was lovely, and the information and assimilation flowed well. After the class, I made more notes and minor changes to the teaching format. I am still finding that learning is ongoing and the changes continuous. It is a constant joy and a continuous adventure. I gave my first talk that fall at East West Bookstore (a great support and resource for all things spiritual in the Seattle area). My first official class followed that talk. The response from those who attended was so gratifying I felt like I could fly! I have continued to grow from each class I give.

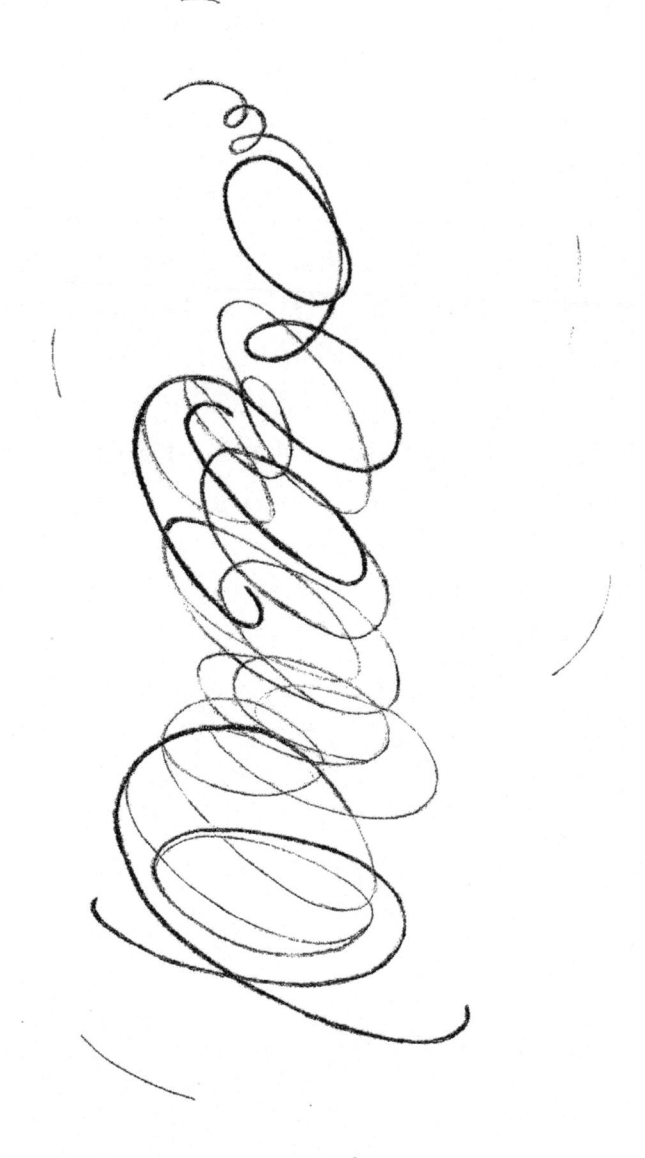

....Energy!

CHAPTER 9

ENERGY

Energy is literally everywhere. Everything on this earth is composed of energy, and energy is vibration. What makes one thing different from another is simply the rate of vibration. People, for example, vibrate at a much faster rate than rock. Rock is dense and slow in its vibration, and it has no sense of consciousness in comparison to our fast vibrating, higher-conscious selves. This is a simplistic explanation but fits our needs for this book. Cells, DNA, and all matter are made of energy. The entire universe is made of energy. Having not yet knowingly experienced other dimensions, my guess is that the vibrations of other dimensions are different from those of earth, yet they are still energy. If I were to guess, my sense would be that the energy is different from the fourth dimension and beyond—finer, tighter, and more focused.

Healing energy and vibrational love is under the guidance of Enoch. There are two energy streams, one called Metatrone and the other called Mahatrone. Enoch is sometimes called the Metatrone.

When it comes to universal energy used by humans, most of it comes to us through the Metatrone. Metatrone means: many diffused energies. It is a stream of energy that Reiki and other healing modalities access. Most healing modalities are *diffused* (not as concentrated so they can utilized by our human bodies) through the Metatrone, making it ready for our use. When Reiki was first introduced on Earth, it had all the intensity that the human body could handle. Reiki is still a very viable and important part of our world community, but there are new needs we need to meet. Since each human body is different in its receptivity, compatibility, and needs, it makes sense that we would be provided by God with different levels of energy for different stages in our evolution.

Zimbaté comes to us from the Mahatrone energy. We can define Mahatrone as that which is "great or celestial energy." It is a direct (unfiltered) energy from God. I am not saying that all energy is not from God, it is. What I am saying is that this is stronger and more direct than any energy we have been using in our current lifetime. It is a bump up in vibration. It has a new quality to the vibration that we, as humans, are now ready to embrace and use. The fact that this energy has been given to us by Enoch again means that our human bodies have evolved enough to assimilate and use this higher vibration. It means we have a more advanced and effective addition to our toolbox. This in no way puts down any other modality, in fact, the variety of people in the world calls for a variety of methods and techniques to meet the multitude of needs that arise. Not everyone will be attracted to Zimbaté, and that is perfectly okay, I'm just happy that you are willing to read about it!

I believe that Zimbaté is the most powerful energy accessible on the planet now. (I am very aware of remarkable healers who seem to defy all known modalities and show astonishing results. In this book I am referring to techniques that are teachable and able to be passed on to others). Zimbaté has one quite distinctive attribute from other modalities. It is pure energy. Reiki is a healing energy. Zimbaté is an energy that can also heal. A very important distinction: it has a broad reach and does not have limitations. *No limitations.* We are only confined by our own thinking, Zimbaté has no limitations. The possibilities stretch my thinking, which is such a good thing! How we talk about Zimbaté in ten years' time could be totally different and so elevated compared to now. What an adventure.

People have asked where the word Zimbaté comes from and about its meaning. The definition of the word Zimbaté was given to me in 2011 by Balzar. Zimbaté is a celestial sound vibration. The vibration of the word Zimbaté has been "stepped" down, so that in the third dimension the sound is translated as Zimbaté. Chant the word Zimbaté and see how you respond.

Zimbaté is available and ready for others to learn. I have seen remarkable results in my practice, and I believe that as I enhance my ability to transmit, so will the power of this Mahatrone energy grow through me. It has amazing potential. In the future, as our bodies increase in vibratory rates, so will our abilities to channel this energy. We have just begun to become aware of the possibilities and opportunities that await our growth and understanding.

Healing energy comes in many forms and modalities. Reiki, one of the best known of these healing modalities, uses energy that comes to the practitioner through their crown chakra down to their hands and then transmits to the client.

Zimbaté is similar in that it enters the body in the same way. As powerful energy as Zimbaté is, it enters the body in a gentle and soft way. There is nothing harsh, insensitive, or invasive. Often clients do not feel anything until they come to the realization that their pain has eased or a sense of well-being envelops them. I have found that I will often become aware of a shift before my clients do. There seems to be a time lapse between the body experiencing a change and the person becoming conscious of that change. I guess we need a little time to catch up with ourselves!

My personal understanding of energy has shown that the physical manifestation has thickness, movement, direction, and texture. This can vary depending on the situation of the client and /or the practitioner. Clients can have a sense of the energy in or around their own bodies. There are so many different reasons for different responses that I look upon any physical manifestations as fascinating but not necessarily an indication of the results. Results come from the adjustment or change in the client, not how we got to that point. I do not judge the success of a session by physical or external sensations. There have been times when a session did not obviously appear to be effective from my point of view, yet the client experienced a huge personal shift.

I do feel that external feedback and response are useful in terms of aiding the practitioner to find a pattern of his or her personal body response. Over time and with experience, a practitioner will gain wisdom in how he or she interacts and relates to the energy. However, that does not necessarily guide you in what response the client is having. Every single person who works with energy will have a unique response. There is no standard that states one response is better than another is. We are all individuals, and our relationship to energy is individual. Interestingly, there are great healers who have almost no awareness or physical response to energy.

It's time for a little experiment. Let's see if we can demonstrate a tangible example of using this energy. Briskly rub your hands together a few times until they get hot, and then pull them apart about two to three inches. Move your hands up, down, and in circles with your hands facing each other. Can you feel energy there? Perhaps heaviness? Thickness, for lack of a better word? Practice a few times. Rub your hands together, and place them over the food you are about to eat, a plant, another person. Play with the energy. Give it a chance to broaden your awareness of your surroundings. Like many things, practice is key, and you may eventually develop your ability to sense this energy, so even if you're not immediately successful, stick with it until you feel something tangible.

Years ago I desperately wanted to develop a connection with crystals. For two years I studied, touched, and held crystals. I felt nothing, but I just kept at it. One day in a shop, I picked up a small cluster of Washington State clear crystals and, *bam!* I felt something wonderful! Excited by my newfound connection I continued to play with crystals and began to use them creatively. As my enchantment waned, I realized that, as fun as it was playing with my new awareness, crystals and the energy they channel were just another addition to my toolbox. Yes, on occasion, I call on that particular energy, but I learned that it was just one of many means of connection and communication and to not get too wrapped up in it. Sometimes we can be distracted by these abilities and lose sight of the bigger picture. On occasion these metaphysical sidebars can become all consuming. We must never lose the desire to experiment and explore, but we should keep in mind balance and common sense.

We have all experienced feeling inexplicably uncomfortable in a room, in a situation, or simply in the company of another person. We are not sure why this is so. Maybe the hairs stand up on the backs of our necks; we feel panicky and can't wait to get out of the situation. We feel tremendous relief when it is over. That is an example of feeling some aspects of the energy available to us if we pay special attention. If you increase your everyday awareness, you may surprise yourself as to how well you can tap into the energy that surrounds you. Our ability to perceive or read this energy helps keep us safe and gives us feedback in all kinds of life situations. We all do it, all day, most people are just unaware of it!

Seeing energy is as real as feeling it. There are many books written on sensing and seeing energy for you to explore if you wish to know more. Here is a simple exercise for you to try. Hold your hands away from your body. Look at the palm of your hands, and face a light-colored wall. Diffuse and soften your eyesight by looking through your hands at the wall. Continue to look for a couple of minutes through your hands. You will see a light blue or white color shimmering around your fingers. This is a part of your aura, which is part of your own personal energy field. How lovely is that!

Increasing your knowledge is always a good thing, and energy is a barely studied field. I encourage you to experiment while increasing your awareness of energy in your everyday life. Energy, and our response to it, is a fundamental, ever-present constant in our lives, whether we are aware of it or not. Increasing your attention to this perpetual interplay will increase your ability to sense and feel energy. Focusing your efforts will broaden your competence and increase your scope of understanding of yourself, others, and the world around you.

....LOVE

CHAPTER 10

WHO IS ZIMBATÉ FOR?

I firmly believe that anyone can benefit from taking a Zimbaté class. Age, life experience, or previous experience in other teachings, none of it matters. Reasons for attending a class are as varied as the individuals who choose to do so. I have yet to find someone in a class who did not belong, if someone is not meant to be there then something seems to happen that day that prevents them from attending.

Is there a divine plan at work here? Absolutely! I believe that everyone who partakes in one of my free lectures is there by divine arrangement, *their* divinity. Does that mean that everyone goes on to take the class? No. We all have free will, and depending on your current life situation, sometimes the timing simply does not work. On the other hand, a person who does attend might pass on information that will make a difference to a friend. Or a person may hear something that triggers a change in a course of action later on down the road. There are infinite possibilities and infinite outcomes. I don't believe in accidents, so if you and I are together in a room there *is* a reason. Does it have to be heavy and serious? Certainly not. And often we may never know the "why," but I do trust that, with the proper intent, we have a chance to make a difference. That is unquestionably true for me. I do my best to watch for these happenings.

In the fall of 2007, I had a full class, and one of the attending students asked if she could include a friend. I responded without thinking: "No, we are full...we just don't have the space...." She continued to plead her friend's case, which aroused my antenna. I asked to meet the friend. During our chat a couple more issues around the friend's attendance came up, and I decided to release the decision—if it were intended that she be there, she would find a way to attend. She did, and since that first class, she has been one of my students of whom I am most proud.

I could so easily have lost that opportunity for growth—hers and mine. She brings a lot to my life; she has been a lovely gift. Do I catch every such opportunity? I wish I could say yes, but I do try to be aware and present for opportunities that may occur, and I do the best I can to remember that lesson. Remembering our lessons is all that Zimbaté ever asks of us. And as for the potential learning moments we might miss, lamenting or beating ourselves up for missing them doesn't achieve anything positive. Zimbaté reminds us to be self-forgiving and self-loving in all situations.

During my last trip to England, I was asked what the requirements for attending classes were. My answer was, "You need to be breathing!" I was being a little flippant, but a person's past knowledge or experience really is irrelevant. Sometimes previous knowledge is useful, but, equally, a blank canvas can be just as good a starting point, sometimes better.

One of the remarkable aspects of Zimbaté is its simplicity. For me, God does not complicate life with a lot of rules to trip you up. Rules and pitfalls are human foibles. Zimbaté is straightforward and very clear in its message, and for me this clarity speaks volumes for its authenticity. There is little to memorize and learn, as most of Zimbaté's message is intuitive and, therefore, flexible in application.

One of the greatest joys in teaching a class lies in witnessing how people react to receiving the energy. It can be just what one student thought it would be. When they first heard about Zimbaté, they might have got a very clear picture about how Zimbaté would fit into their life. But another student might be totally surprised by the results. Some come to a class with no real goal in mind. Over the course of the classes, as I check in with students, I love hearing their stories about what they are doing with Zimbaté and how it has affected their lives. Here are some responses from people I have encountered that I'd like to share with you:

> When I first met Carolyn, I was initially very skeptical about what I was hearing in relation to Zimbaté. I have a degree in biology and worked as a postgraduate researcher. My thoughts ran along the line of "not another new healing system that claims miraculous results." Carolyn defeated my skepticism almost immediately with a short demonstration, which resulted in a massive energy shift within my heart chakra. From that moment on, I was intrigued enough to take up Carolyn's kind offer to teach me Zimbaté. I have been teaching Reiki for over ten years and have trained in several energy modalities, and I can honestly say that Zimbaté is in a league of its own.

My first client has terminal cancer and I work with him once a week. He has four tumors, three in his spinal column and one on his second from top rib on the right side. He has been undergoing chemotherapy on the highest dose they can give. He had a scan after the third week I had been working with him. The assistant consultant cried while viewing the results, as all three tumors in his spine had shrunk beyond detection. The one on his ribs is still there but has slowed down. The hospital could not believe the results: it shocked my client and amazed me. I believe that Zimbaté helped facilitate and enhance my client's capacity to heal and thus helped him to clear his three spinal tumors.

Thank you, Carolyn, for sharing this amazing modality with the world and myself.

Paul Evans

I am a perfect example of what happens to your mind and body when you spend sixty-eight years wearing out your body parts. I have survived throat cancer surgery and radiation, two knee replacements, and a stomach that needed reconstruction. Not only am I a survivor of those major surgeries, but I continue to have an active wonderful quality of life, which is the purpose of this endorsement of Zimbaté.

In the process of recoveries, I used western medical surgeons, doctors of naturopathic medicine, and Carolyn's sessions of Reiki and Zimbaté. It is not possible to say what type of medicine contributed to what part in the recoveries, but I know for sure that I recovered faster and with a better quality of life than any of my friends who have suffered similar problems did.

Carolyn was able to visit me for both hands-on and hands-off sessions, and there is no doubt she was able to put me into a higher level of calm and healing than the nurse who woke me up to take a pill in the hospital.

Dan from Maui

Since having experienced my initiation and receiving Zimbaté the subtle shifts, such as in my diet to increased abundance of raw food, deeper sleep, and more energy during the day, feeling lighter in my body. And my sixth sense is more finely tuned.

Zimbaté is becoming a way of life; by integrating my intentions I am becoming more aware of us being as one, of seeing more of my intentions being realized as I become more connected with my higher purpose. And as we approach 2012, I am so grateful to have found Zimbaté and to be working with people in a new and dynamic way.

Much love and light, Sam xx

I read about Zimbaté in the Centenary issue of Kindred Spirit. There was a deep sense of familiarity about Zimbaté, like an old memory at the back of my mind, so much so I called Carolyn then and there and invited her to the UK. I have not looked back since.

Zimbaté imbues every aspect of my life, subtle yet present in everything I do. There is a sense of growing on a physical, mental, and spiritual level. It is subtle, almost indiscernible, yet like a kaleidoscope, where one subtle change alters the whole picture.

Jonathan Tarr

Quite simply, Zimbaté healing is pure unconditional love.

Siwan Quinn Bratton

...Intention!

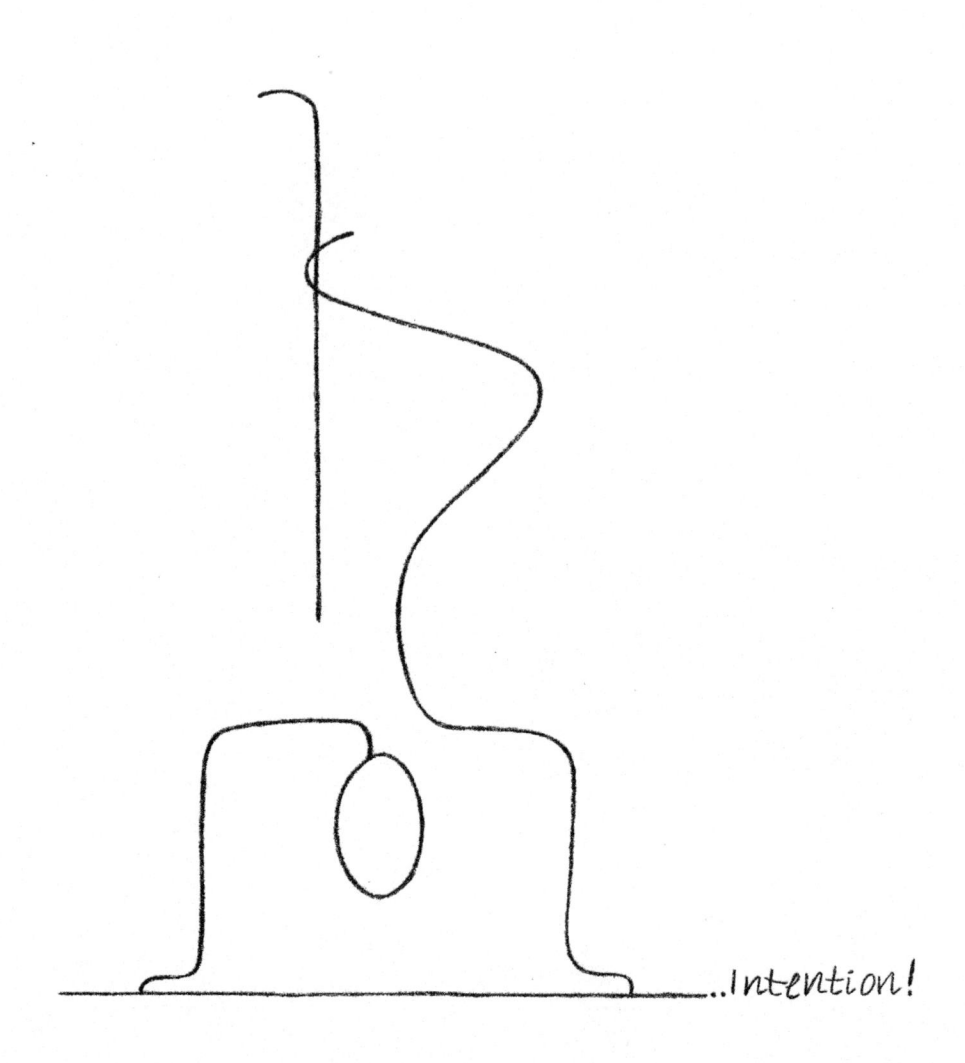

CHAPTER 11

THE POWER OF INTENT

One area of working with Zimbaté is not flexible or negotiable—*intent and motive*- they are so important I cannot emphasize the importance of intent and motive enough, so let's talk about them.

It does not matter if you forget the order of things, mispronounce a word, or leave a piece of the protocol out. All these things are taught in class. The most important part of any kind of energy work is intent. Actually, I think that pure intent is vital to living a life of integrity. So, what is intent? Intent is one's aim or purpose; the state of one's mind when one carries out an action. Motive is the emotion, desire, or psychological need that incites one to action. First the intent comes and then the motive for the action. At this level of healing, with such a high vibration, your pure intent and motive is crucial.

An example of *im*pure intent is seeing Zimbaté as a money making exercise, a view which might fool one into thinking that they are humbly dedicating their working life to the service of others. Their public face would be one of compassion, but as time went on, the money might not be coming fast enough, so this person might raise the price of their classes or cut corners in their teaching. The core values would come to mean less, and they would justify this from their ego-centered position. Yet, it is possible for them to sincerely believe their humble public face—self-delusion is powerful. Unless you have experienced the difference between pure intent and ego-based intent, and spent quality time learning who you are, you might find it difficult to know the difference.

What is the role the ego plays in intent? It is actually the major player, so understanding our ego is key. The ego is seated in the sacral chakra and is divided into two distinct parts. The third-dimensional ego (EGO = earth guidance only) is only concerned with external control. It is attracted to control and has a need to feel important. It seeks power in the world and power over others. Lots of us have control issues, and I guess to an extent it's a self-preservation instinct—a need to express one's individuality freely and part of our human weakness. We all have an ego, and it can be so clever in its drive to be in charge and preserve itself, that it can fool us too. I don't mean to imply that the ego is a separate being, it is of course just one facet of our selves, but for the purposes of getting the message across it can be helpful to think of the external ego as something we need to be wary of and keep in check. Actually, the ideal would be to eliminate the external ego. We need to be vigilant in assessing our true intent and understanding where we are on our path. Vigilance is part of being present.

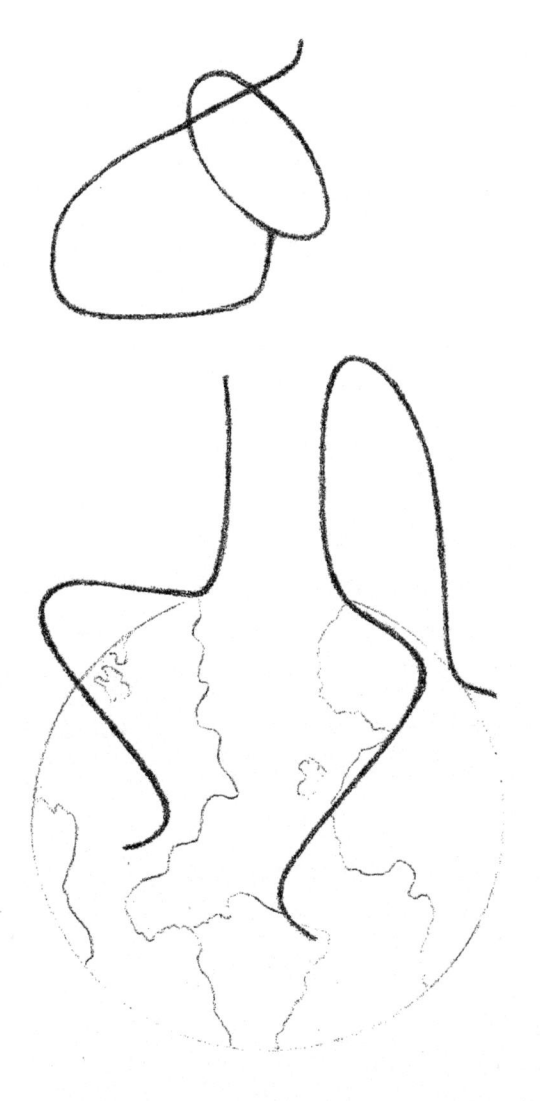

..... _Earth_ _Guidance_ _only_

But the ego is not all about external power, internal power is the place we strive to grow and nurture. Internal power is having the strength to live with integrity, and internal power comes from knowing ourselves deeply. The ego is not inherently bad or evil; it is simply that, when fed inappropriately, its negative aspects thrive. The internal ego is the consciousness of "I can," "I will," and "I know," so it is important to nurture the ego with pure intent and motives. When you come from a solid place within, you have peace and harmony in your world. There is flow in your life. Yes, issues come up and problems still appear, but you are able to meet them with serenity and grace. Our goal is to promote personal empowerment and eliminate our need for external use of power—to cherish and encourage our own ability to recognize the difference between external and internal power. Recognizing a pure heart demands internal understanding of both the positive and the negative within ourselves and demands the recognition, without judgment, of how we best deal with both aspects.

It can be so easy to convince ourselves of good intention and integrity without bothering to look within ourselves. We all, as per the human condition, have a touch of arrogance. Don't get caught up in such third-dimensional drama. Enoch, who you will remember from our earlier discussion, is the patriarch of our planet, known as the man with two brains. This was in reference to his conscious action of first filtering information though his heart to determine if he held the information in true intent and had integrity. Enoch always questioned the intent and motive behind the information. If it felt pure, he would allow his brain to process the information.

He was a wise scholar and a man who displayed impeccable judgment. Not a bad act to follow! My intention is simply to emphasize the importance of integrity within any energy work. For those who feel unsure of their underlying intent, you have a fallback. Your real heart and true intent is known by those who guide Zimbaté and its practitioners from the unseen world, feel secure in that knowledge.

.... me and my guide

CHAPTER 12

MEET YOUR GUIDE

Another special aspect of Zimbaté is receiving your guide. The guides will be beings from the Great White Brotherhood who have impeccable credentials! You will make contact with them during a dedicated meditation in your class. Yes, *everyone* in the class will leave with a guide—I promise!

Your guide will work with you whenever you ask for assistance. You have the opportunity to develop a wonderful relationship. You will feel like you have gained a new best friend, a friend who looks out for your best interests in a way you have never experienced before. When you call on your guide, a physical response in your body lets you know your guide is with you.

Your guide will work with your client, through you, to produce the best possible outcome. If you do not use Zimbaté with others, your guide will work solely with you. You can call on your guide to assist you in whatever task you might have. Your guide is there for you; you and your guide are a team. Now remember, your guide also has a responsibility to integrity. For this team to work in perfect harmony you must both be in alignment with pure intent and motive. You will know when you and your guide are in that pure alignment. I personally feel a warm glow when I call upon my guide; I feel especially well loved, and I know you will too.

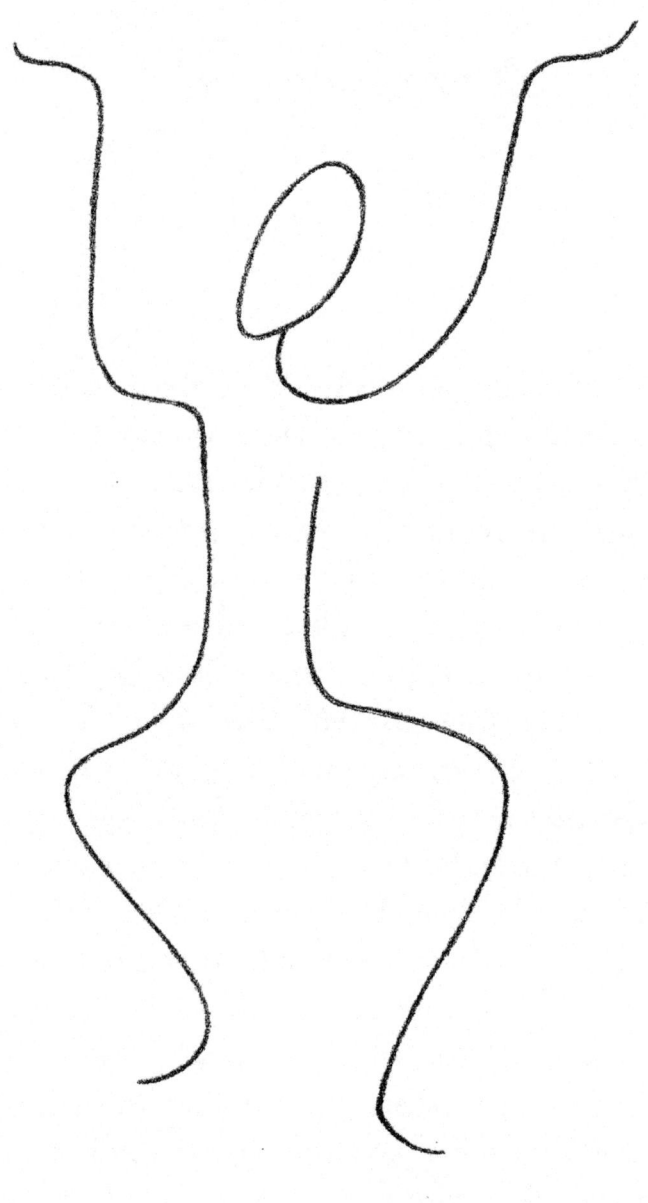

..... oh Well!

CHAPTER 13

MORE BENEFITS

From my point of view, addressing personal issues and working through them is a priority for everyone, practitioner and client alike. The more you can do for *you*, the more you can genuinely do for others. Just as the more you give to others, the more you receive. To that end, Zimbaté provides you with several solid tools for your toolbox.

You will have a guide with whom your relationship will develop and deepen over time. You will have various techniques at your disposal that will help you to address specific areas of concern. You will have a chant that will center you and balance your chakras. You will be able to use images and color to aid your practice. You will find it increasingly natural to do daily work with your own body. A lovely point to remember is that when you work with someone else, the energy that flows through your body to theirs to address their issues will also address your issues—it's a relationship of perfect symbiosis. After I have conducted a session, I find myself both invigorated and rested. Using Zimbaté always feels like a blessing.

Once you have chosen to let Zimbaté become part of your life, you open a world of possibilities. Aspects of our lives that do not serve us tend to fall away without discomfort. For example, a toxic relationship that has become habitual can gradually fade and no longer be a part of your life. Even if you find the concept too painful to bear right now, if it is not right for you, your life view has an opportunity to see new horizons. Zimbaté can assist you in meeting your needs and dealing with the pain of change. Maybe your living arrangement is no longer satisfactory, but you have not been able to find anything better. Then, unexpectedly, someone has a suggestion that helps facilitate a move. You despair of ever getting a job you love and are surprised when an opportunity for work comes seemingly from nowhere.

I am not saying that Zimbaté is an instant gratification button. What I am saying is that having Zimbaté in our lives allows us to open our awareness and draw positive solutions closer, solutions that always exist for us but which we may normally struggle to see. Then, with gentleness, Zimbaté will assist us in changing. Often, when I have reunions with previous classes, and I ask how students' lives have changed in the past year or so, I hear about some major life changes. Yet it never appears to be full of drama or trauma; it just happens so naturally, so organically, that some students don't even see how significant that year has been. That is the beauty of Zimbaté.

People and situations can, and do, change for the better. You can use Zimbaté to sensitize yourself to what is toxic and uncomfortable in your environment and work together toward change. I see Zimbaté as a partnership. You can't sit on the couch and expect change to happen for you, but if you have pure intent and put forth effort, Zimbaté will reciprocate—we are all just energy after all. Your guide and those who are available to you are most eager to support you in having a full and positive life experience. Remember that, it is important.

I have found that when I am in the positive flow, with trust in my life, very little goes amiss. Whether it is getting to my appointments on time or having enough money, I find there is an ease to each day. You know about that small voice in your head that talks to you. It is vital that you learn to listen to that voice. That inner voice is quiet and is easy to miss or ignore. However, your small voice is also smart and has your best interests at heart. It does everything it can to help you avoid daily pitfalls. Your inner voice may push you in the right direction by bringing to your mind a familiar name, and you then know it is important to call that person. It might be a thought that you have to take a different route to work and, as a result, perhaps you unknowingly avoid a traffic accident. Frustrated that you can't find your keys in the morning? Maybe those five minutes at home saved you from disaster. Who knows, life is mysterious and infinitely wonderful in its complexity. You get my point. That voice is a personal guide and can contribute hugely to the success of your life. Zimbaté has nurtured my ability to hear that small voice better. Do I always listen? No, but I am getting better!

I've had some pretty big dreams in these last few years, and they are becoming my reality. It is through my work with Balzar and Zimbaté that I have been in the right space to allow all these good things to happen. I have had a great many adventures I could not have dreamed up, and I am grateful I was open enough to permit them into my life. Permit abundance, and abundance will be yours. Unlimited opportunities and possibilities are for the taking if you'll have them, good or bad, and much of that you will decide for yourself through intent and motive.

Is there one secret that will change your life for the better? Not that I know of. It is a combination of everything that is offered to you. We pick and choose to the best of our abilities, learn what we can, and keep moving forward. That is all we can do. Sometimes it is hard not to judge our past and wish we had done things differently. There is no mileage in regret. My best advice for a happy and fulfilled life is to do the best you can each day, and then, "Oh, well," covers everything else!

CHAPTER 14

THE STUDENT

Students are drawn to a Zimbaté class for many reasons and they use their acquired knowledge in many ways. It does not matter how you end up using your knowledge as long as it is with good intent. You may use Zimbaté with yourself only or perhaps use it to benefit your family and friends. You may feel drawn to use it in a professional setting and charge money for the service. You may already practice another modality and find that you are looking for an additional tool to enhance that profession. Don't discount the fact that how you start out may not be the place you end up! I'm a great example of that!

One of the greatest gifts of Zimbaté is its flexibility. It is a stand-alone modality, or it can support and enrich your current practice and / or modality. If you are a massage therapist, try firing up Zimbaté at the beginning of a session, and then continue to work as you normally would. I'm sure you will get the best results you have ever had and will no doubt have the happiest of clients.

CHAPTER 15

THE PRACTITIONER

Healers are really a conduit or facilitator for the energy. It is *the clients* who do the healing or change. They have free will and at all times are in charge of their lives and their life paths. We have the honor of being present to assist by facilitating the flow of the energy and helping support the transformation. People receive healing by the combination of the energy of Zimbaté and their own intent and needs. I have encountered many people who do not believe that they have the power to change and influence their own lives in this way. Often they do not want to face the responsibility that acknowledging their participation requires. Sometimes they just do not know enough to understand. This gives the healer an opportunity to educate and help others understand the roles we can each play in empowering our own health and wellbeing.

Clients will frequently thank me for "healing" them. This generally is meant to thank me for my time and presence. "I" personally, the human me, do not make changes in another human being. I simply provide the energy, a safe environment, and the encouragement for transformation. The client receives the energy and uses it for his or her higher good. Practitioners play an important personal role in that the clearer their physical, emotional, mental, and spiritual bodies are, the cleaner the vessel they become, and the more space they make available for energy to flow within them. Let me explain.

When an individual has issues, problems, and blocks in his or her life there is less space for positivity to thrive. Problems exist not only in your physical body but also within your emotional, mental, and spiritual bodies. We can think of problems as dense energy blocking our natural flow, weighing us down. Problems create a density in our body that is not present in us when we are in balance, our natural state of being. Have you ever resolved an issue and, as a consequence, felt lighter? You have literally become lighter in a sense, the density has been replaced with a lighter, more positive, higher vibrational energy. When you liberate issues, you become lighter, and your body rises to a higher vibration. When your body can handle a higher vibration from the universe, the tenor of the work you do with others amplifies. When you decrease your density, everyone and everything benefits—especially you!

People who are clear vessels are better receptors for information. If you are confused and have muddy thinking and feelings about your own life, it is difficult to process and make sense of someone else's life; your perceptive filters (how we process information) are clouded. Discernment and sensitivity are valuable assets in a person, but they take practice and lots of self-awareness.

The same can be said for listening—that special art that, in reality, is little practiced! Most of us use the time when others are talking to plan what we will say next. We, therefore, never *really* listen to the other person in the true sense of listening, which is (to use a dictionary reference) "to attend

....expansion

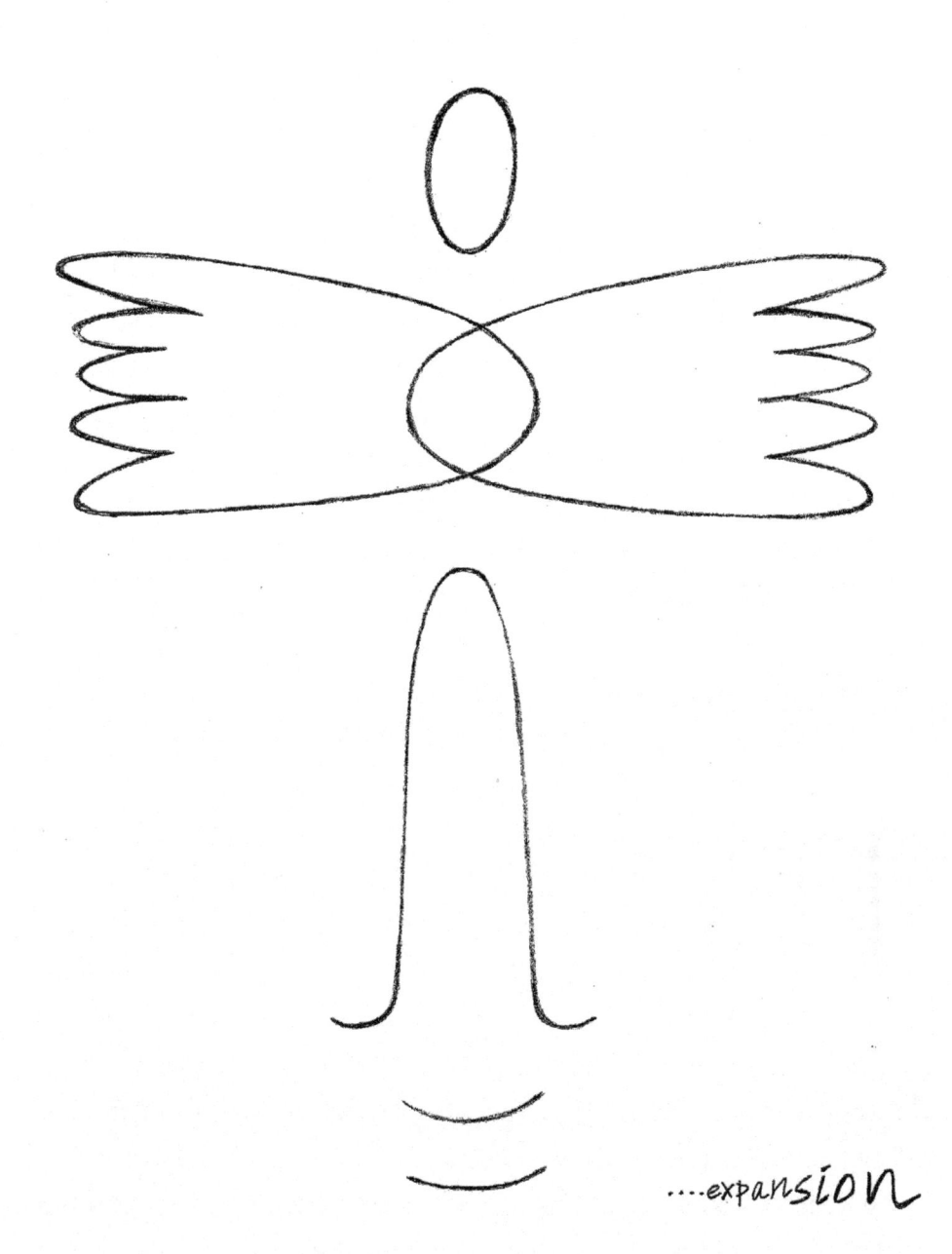

closely for the *sole purpose of hearing*." People who are truly present for others offer them a real gift. *Really* being listened to brings joy to people in ways they often don't experience from a simple conversation. To feel that another person fully understands and empathizes is simply priceless. Give true listening a try. During the next few conversations you engage in, try to participate by saying very little. Focus on what others are saying, and do not let your own responses get in the way of your listening. When you do respond, really respond to what others have said. Stay present with them, do not make it about you, and you will see how difficult it can be! Learning the art of listening is a skill that will endlessly benefit you in all aspects of your life, not just as a practitioner.

Additional important skills will set you apart from other practitioners. What follows is by no means comprehensive but a helpful exploration of some of the qualities so often overlooked. Remember, anything that you face, overcome, and conquer will add to the quality of your life and those you serve.

As a therapist, I do not try to influence a client to change treatment plans or behaviors to fit my beliefs. For example, I have never told a person with cancer they should forego conventional medicine. It is his or her life and decision. I will give my own opinion if asked, but I'm sure to reiterate that my opinion is simply that, my opinion. I am not a trained medical professional and, therefore, I feel it is important to do only what I am skilled to do and that is to facilitate the energy and be a supportive presence.

Without proper training, I feel concern when a practitioner tells a client that he or she sees, feels, or hears information about the client's health and wellbeing. There is a mysterious and rarely knowable space between the ego and our perceptive filters, but our ego is strong and fools us into overlooking this fact. One must be aware of client vulnerability and the possible consequences of any comments you choose to make upon a client's life. If you have experiences to share that could be valuable to a client, share if it feels right after careful consideration, but please remember to focus on clear intent in all that you do. One of the most important skills you can acquire is to be able to think and act outside of your ego—that is much harder than it sounds.

For the same reasons as just mentioned, I am equally hesitant to give a diagnosis. Generally, whatever information I receive during a session with a client stays with me, but I choose to keep it there because I do not know how relevant the information is to the present moment (more on that point in a minute). Unless you have medical training, I don't believe you should give out medical advice.

When you start to work with healing energy and observe the changes that occur with clients, it can be heady stuff. Remember that this is the domain of that tricky ego, and do not let it lead you astray. I once touched a client and immediately had a vision of her recovering from surgery in a hospital bed. However, it wasn't until a whole five years later that she had surgery. Can you imagine the fear I could have created for her if I had shared my vision those five years earlier? The surgery was totally unrelated to anything she or I could have known about at the time of our session. Although it was a strong and ultimately accurate vision, it simply wasn't relevant or helpful at that time, and I was right to keep it to myself.

Another example of a practitioner misconstruing the intensity of an experience happened during a class in my home. My eldest daughter, Darcy, was lying on the massage table during a session break. One of the other students came up to her and started working on her back. There was a lot of energy flowing, and the student was quite naturally caught up in all the action. He told my daughter that she had a problem that could be a serious medical issue. Darcy didn't say anything to her fellow student, but she told me what he had said to her. Darcy explained that she was suffering from severe menstrual cramps that day. Well, that would be enough to explain the level of energy activity in her body! Imagine if Darcy was in a vulnerable state and left that session believing she had a serious medical issue. The placebo effect has its own mysterious power, and the consequences of such a belief could have been detrimental to her health. This occurrence opened up a perfect space to discuss with the class the importance of censoring our feedback.

Having said all this, Zimbaté works beautifully alongside other healing modalities and can easily complement conventional medical protocol; they are not in opposition. In fact, the opposite can be true; surely, it is better to cover all angles to see what works best for you in your current situation. I want to encourage practitioners to nurture a warm and successful relationship with those you work with, so use common sense and think before you speak. It is okay to share your insights with others if you are present and aware of what you say and act only with integrity. Personally, there is seldom greater joy in my life than when I am practicing Zimbaté. Given all we have just discussed, your practice should foremost be a joyful experience for all involved. Zimbaté is pure, loving, and nurturing, free from ego and ulterior motives, and, therefore, a rare pleasure to experience.

CHAPTER 16

THE CLIENT

Anyone can receive Zimbaté. You do not need to have special training, know anything, or do anything to make it "work." It is not about thinking, it is about feeling. On your first session, please ask the questions, and get the information you need to feel at ease. Be in a comfortable position that promotes relaxation, your experience should be a pleasant one!

Let me dispense with one issue right now. You have free will. Use it. Don't let anyone force you to do something you are not comfortable doing. This is all about you, not what someone else wants. Do not do something simply because "someone" says you must. Don't be manipulated. During a session of energy healing you are in charge. You are the one who is using the energy and making changes. The person working with you is providing the fuel, but you are in the driver's seat. You can go confidently into a session knowing that you are not passively turning yourself over for someone to do something to you; you are the active ingredient! Having said that, the practitioner expects nothing of you, so just feel at ease, and do only what fits with this feeling.

Here is what happens when you receive energy. Your higher self knows what it needs and which needs to meet first. You may seek healing for help managing back pain but find that another area of your body (spiritual, mental, or emotional) has a greater need. You don't control this in your human way; your higher self takes over that task. All you need to do is relax and let it flow.

Depending on what your body requires, one session may address several areas. I have found that our bodies (physical, spiritual, mental, and emotional) are capable of infinite changes in each session or, in some cases, not much change at all. This will vary depending upon the severity of the need, the condition of the client's body, and all the other factors that make us different each and every day! Sometimes a little break in the session is all the time your body needs to adjust. You can trust your therapist will know the timing. When your body has done all it will in one session, the energy simply ceases to flow.

One hard and fast rule is that with any problem, the sooner you get help the easier it is to resolve. Chronic problems that have plagued you for years can take more time to heal than an injury you address immediately. As with most things in life, using your common sense goes a long way.

Zimbaté has proven to be of tremendous help when working with cancer and other serious illnesses. It will aid in relieving the illness and its root cause as well as assisting your ability to cope with the situation and its stressful side effects. Outcomes can and will vary, but you can be assured of positive results; they just might not be what you would expect. In the twenty-five years that I have been practicing, all my clients have had results in one way or another.

One woman came to me with a pain in her upper back. The session from my point of view was very successful, but not so much from hers. There was a remarkable amount of energy being used by her body, and I was pleased for this client. When we finished, she was not happy. She still had pain in her back. My thought at the time was that she might have averted cancer, a breakdown, or some other unseen problem. It was unfortunate that she was not open to other possibilities, but at least her higher self was open! This energy work is not for just the big stuff in your life. It is for *all* of the parts. In fact, sometimes the small stuff is just as important in helping to keep you centered and well balanced.

Clients often have concerns about their response to a session. They often ask, "If I can't feel anything, is anything happening?" Yes, Zimbaté works regardless of what we feel. Some people have a greater sensitivity to energy than others do, but the sensitivity does not necessarily affect results. Sometimes it is just a matter of practice and patience. Other times we will feel the results in our bodies hours or even days later. If the issue being worked with is mental or emotional you might not gain awareness of a shift until a situation arises that would normally trigger a certain response; your new response is different, and change has indeed occurred without you realizing.

There is no way to determine how a session will go. I once worked with a cancer patient every day for months and found that each session was a little different. The energy will address the predominant issue in the moment, and as we know, life and our needs are in constant flux. Some sessions may feel more significant than others, but you will learn to take an interest in each experience without judgment.

Acute conditions sometimes, ironically, can be the most easily dealt with. I guess the need is greatest and most obvious. Working with someone directly after surgery can eliminate a lot of the need for pain medications. Zimbaté can often greatly reduce the time needed to heal a wound and at the same time speed up the removal of anesthesia from the body. You may not want to work with someone during surgery unless the medical team is completely on board with the program. Energy healing can create changes in vital signs that could cause undue concern if the medical team does not know what to expect.

I have a story of my own. In 2010 I personally experienced two surgeries, one of which was to repair a severely injured rotator cuff. My doctor prescribed me ninety strong narcotic-based painkillers and continually asked me if I needed more, based on his findings that such surgery often called for patients to continue pain relief treatment for two to four months. I took the medication for three days before feeling well enough to stop treatment. My doctor questioned my lack of pain in disbelief.

My other surgery, a hysterectomy and bladder repair, was very easy. I had a friend come to meet with me in the hospital and do Zimbaté. I used no pain relief at all until the nurse and I had words. She insisted that I take pain relief to get me home, and I refused. I eventually realized the nurse was not going to give in, and I wanted to get home, so I agreed. I learned a valuable lesson that day. The pill made me sick, so I had to stay in the hospital longer. I worked hard to eliminate the medication from my body as fast as possible. I took no more pain relief, and the rest of my recovery was easy, with no pain or complications.

Another interesting dynamic is that some of us come into this world to experience pain, illness, or other afflictions for reasons we may never know. Life is mysterious, and we cannot always anticipate or understand its path. We may need to suffer a certain affliction in order to experience growth we would not normally be open to otherwise. A certain amount of faith will bode well for us. Zimbaté will not mask issues. It will deal only with what our higher selves are ready to alleviate, for whatever purpose. You certainly will still benefit from Zimbaté on some level, but maybe not in the way your human self hoped to benefit. When you are ready to reverse your illness and when the underlying issues resolve, you will make fabulous progress. We can never know the path of another. As healers, we can simply be compassionate, understanding and allow people their path without judgment. As clients, we can only follow our intuition and our hearts.

CHAPTER 17

BITS AND BOBS

Choice surrounds us. This is one of life's advantages as well as one of its challenges. Choices are many and wide-ranging, as are spiritual paths. You may wonder how to choose a teacher and a modality or what is right for you. You may wonder how you will know it works. The questions can be endless and the answers confusing. I would like to share some thoughts and suggestions with you to help you along your journey. The final decisions are up to you and you only. Exercise your gift of free will.

With my experience in the field of healing, I've seen a lot, heard much more, and done some of it. There is much that is good and some that is not quite what it should be. If you are drawn to an activity that is new to you, research it. The Internet is a helpful tool as long as you take into account there is no one validating the material. This is at the same time one of the best and one of the worst points about the Internet; anyone can say anything he or she likes, and it is there for anyone to see. However, this does make it a great place to test your sense of discernment. Read the material and filter it first though your heart. Be like Enoch. How did you feel after reading the article? Did it ring true for you? Consult all sources you have available, and take notice of the feedback. When you have gathered enough information, check in with yourself. How do you now feel? Apprehensive? Enthusiastic? Never underestimate your body's response; it is sharing valid information with you.

Next, I would talk with the practitioner or someone with knowledge of the practitioner. Personally, I often find myself contacted by a prospective client or student. Ask the practitioner anything you wish; there are no wrong questions. Pay close attention to the answers. Don't be one of those people who are so busy formulating questions they don't hear the answers—the lessons learned earlier about truly listening will stand you in good stead here. If you are happy with the answers and feel the person is honest, respectful, and has integrity, go for it. If you are the practitioner, be patient and really listen to the questions. They can tell you a lot about the person. Remember the client is of the essence here; really be there for him or her.

We can view free will as a valuable safeguard. It protects us from manipulation if we know how to recognize it. No one can manipulate you without your permission. Don't be afraid to challenge a belief or practice. I've been confronted a fair amount, and I actually welcome being challenged in my thinking. I am secure in my knowledge base and my practice, so being defensive is not an issue for me. I am not afraid to say, "I don't know, I'll give it some thought and get back to you." Thinking things through before answering is far wiser than responding with something you are unsure of. There is an important difference between questioning with a positive intent (to learn) and questioning with ego (to antagonize, humiliate, or to simply show off). Most teachers will sense the intent behind a question and answer accordingly.

Before a session take a moment to become comfortable with your surroundings, the practitioner, and your body. Take comfort in the fact that you are the master of your own destiny, and you can leave at any time. It is important here to consider the difference between normal levels of anxiety in any new situation and levels of anxiety that signal discomfort on a deeper level.

Do you feel better after a session? Different? Often there are no immediate discernable changes, but there are times when you may have a profound experience. It really doesn't matter. I have never had a session with anyone who did not have some kind of shift or change, however subtle. Often you and I will not know what change has occurred, but something will have happened. Look at it as a gift just waiting to be received at a later date.

No one person can have an identical response to someone else because we are all as complex and as individual as the energy in use. There are no absolute answers to any issue, injury, or disease. People will respond differently because their needs and intents will be uniquely theirs. Sometimes you come into this life with lessons to learn, and these lessons can involve facing tough issues that you may or may not be ready to deal with. In those cases, your sessions may feel ineffectual. My experience is that there is change, growth, and forward movement every time you receive healing energy to your body. Sometimes, in the moment, you might wonder, but later you may see an amazing result, or you may remain unaware of any change. There is a certain amount of trust needed in yourself and in the process.

I have experienced new responses to familiar situations and had no idea when the change in me had occurred. I'm just grateful that the change did happen. Changes do not have to be hard or painful. Actually, the results of Zimbaté are often effortless and simple, but one exception can be an acute physical injury. When you immediately activate Zimbaté, there will generally be pain while healing occurs, but Zimbaté can render the injury pain free in a short amount of time. The sooner you start to work on any problem, the easier and faster the healing will be. I have burnt my hands several times, and although it is painful working on the area at the time, within minutes, the redness and pain go away, and I have experienced no blistering or discomfort later.

There is no need for any prior experience or knowledge before having a session or taking a class in Zimbaté. Sitting next to someone in a class who knows the language, who talks the talk, can be intimidating, but that is no guarantee they can walk the walk. Rest assured a person's integrity and clear intent makes him or her shine, not the show put on. This realization is a great leveler if you are lacking in confidence. In my first Reiki class, I didn't know a thing about energy, I was mystified and confused by what I was hearing, but by the end of the weekend, I had found a whole new way of being and of seeing the world. Don't let your lack of experience keep you from new experiences.

It is difficult to provide absolute answers to the many questions people have about such a new discipline, so the bottom line is research, ask questions, follow your heart and then your head, and trust in yourself. Remember this is supposed to be exciting, life changing, and fun. Do not let yourself feel daunted by new prospects. Give thanks for the gift of finding yourself moving in directions you could have never have anticipated.

I have had some familiarity with people who others could label professional seekers—those who take as many classes and seminars as possible in their search for a magical answer, the meaning of life, or the ultimate key to happiness. I have witnessed that, in their rush from class to class; they can often miss the real value of what is offered. Take things at your own pace, which may be relatively fast or slow in comparison to someone else's. Stay true to yourself by devoting yourself to one or two modalities at a time, take time to apply what you have learned. After working on an idea for a month or so, if it does not fit into your life, it does not fit, at least for now. Be brave enough to move on and credit yourself for giving something a fair chance to integrate into your life. You never know, you may never visit that area again, or it may come back into your life at a later date and at the right time. Expect nothing and pass no judgment.

From my teaching and personal experience, I have learned that once you have vested knowledge, energy, and structure of a modality it requires time for your body and spirit to assimilate it. How it feels in your body after a few months will be very different from those early days. As you continue to assimilate this practice into your daily routine, the energy becomes part of you in your entirety.

When I first took a class in Reiki, it became the base of my practice. I took other classes and checked out new and interesting ideas. In the back of my mind, I always asked the question, "How does this serve me and my practice of Reiki?" So, over time, I have incorporated other techniques into my practice. I don't necessarily use them often, but I appreciate them for being there when I do need something different. Look at your current practice, and see if you can benefit from something new. If this is a first-time experience for you, see how it would fit alongside your lifestyle and dreams for the future. When I first learned about Zimbaté, I quickly came to realize that it was an elevation in vibration and results. As I became comfortable with the techniques, my practice came to depend upon Zimbaté; it had become my new base. My point is that energy has a tendency to adapt and evolve, and we must be open to adapting and evolving in our relationship to it. This is where the greatest gifts lie.

.... Heart Connection
.... Grounding

CHAPTER 18

WHO HEALS?

I cannot emphasize enough how important it is to understand that a practitioner *does not heal*. The person giving the treatment does not "heal" you; he or she is simply a conduit for the energy. As mentioned earlier in this book, the person receiving the treatment is responsible for his or her own healing or changes. I don't like to hear someone say "I can heal you." That smacks of the human ego speaking. By the way, remember what EGO stands for? Earth Guidance Only! That's a nice and grounding way to remember it.

The practitioner plays an important part, but he or she is not the main attraction. I do not believe that the human part of the practitioner does any healing. Those who want to take the credit and be held above others need to take a serious look at their intent, and I would suggest you look carefully at any person who claims credit for energy healing work. When the energy enters your body, it knows where to go. It will address the area of greatest need first. After that, if you can handle additional change, it will flow to secondary needs, be they physical, spiritual, emotional, or mental. I have found that individuals have unique ways of assimilating energy. They can have different levels of tolerance for change, and these can vary from day to day according to the seriousness of the problem. What appears on the outside is not always what is on the inside. We cannot always know what our higher selves need. People will often say, "Thank you for healing me." I don't want to embarrass a client with a lecture about responsibility and job description and will simply say, "You are welcome." But I will have taken time at some point during a session to clarify both my role as well as the client's role within the proceedings, as it is important to understand that energy healing is empowering to the self rather than something that is "done to them" and mysterious. I am happy to receive their thanks because an exchange has taken place, and for that, I am always grateful and humbled.

CHAPTER 19

CLASSES

There are three levels to the class structure of Zimbaté. First degree is the basics. Second degree has advanced techniques, and the third degree is all about being a teacher.

In a first-degree class you will start with a question and answer session, this is important, as I want everyone to be fully comfortable with Zimbaté before we start. First comes an attunement, which is very short and is "open eye." This means you may watch or not. First degree includes two distinct parts to the training, with little to memorize. And with the class notes given to you, there is no need to take notes during class, which allows you to be fully present in the experience and practice of Zimbaté. The class is all about interaction and understanding, so the more you can participate, the better. Class includes methods for you to use with others and techniques to use for your personal growth and development. It is in the first-degree class that you contact and communicate with your guides. Everyone will have a guide; one of the special connections Zimbaté brings to your life. How you develop that relationship is up to you.

Second degree provides advanced techniques, using the energy in new ways. You will learn to share Zimbaté with "distant healing." This is actually doing Zimbaté without having the person, place, or thing with you. Distant healing has no acknowledgement or need for time, distance, or space. Zimbaté comes to us without third-dimension restrictions. You can work in the future or go back to something in the past. You can work with a situation, a relationship, a place, a feeling, with plants, or with animals. You can send energy to people and areas of our planet that are in distress, or you can work with our planet or universe as a whole. Remember the Zimbaté mantra *there are no limitations*.

Third degree gives you a boost in ability with Zimbaté but concentrates mainly on teaching. You have the continuing support of your teacher and practice to develop your skills. When you take a class, you might have a preconceived idea of what you will do with your new knowledge and skills, but be prepared for the unexpected! Be open to this new experience. Let it evolve, and enjoy how it can open and transform all or parts of your life.

You may use Zimbaté in a professional setting while working with others. Alternatively, you may use it with yourself and family. That part does not matter at all. You may be drawn to call on Zimbaté at various times in your future life in different settings. However you use it, be sure that it is a perfect fit for you. Zimbaté may simply support and enhance what you are currently doing, or you might find yourself on a whole new exciting adventure. What it will certainly do is provide support for you in whichever ways you need it and whenever you need it on your wondrous journey through life.

...Now go and have fun!

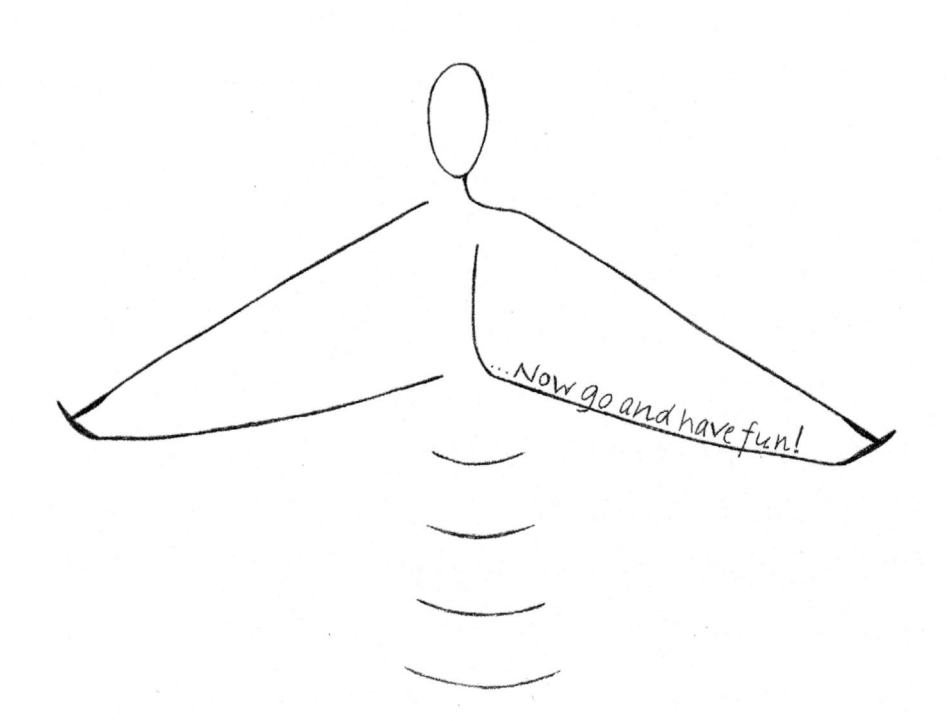

CHAPTER 20

WHERE WE ARE NOW

Since 2006, I have been traveling to England once or twice a year to teach Zimbaté. The response from students and clients has been warm and encouraging. Interest in Zimbaté is growing, and the uses for Zimbaté have diversified beautifully—we are successfully using Zimbaté in detox centers!

In the last couple of years, I have found people whose integrity and intent has matched the criteria for Zimbaté leadership. With their assistance, a new organization is being formed called Zimbaté International. It will be an organization to support *all* who are Zimbaté practitioners and teachers. It is for anyone who wants a sense of community, a place to share ideas, and a place to learn from one another. It will ultimately be a resource for practitioners and clients seeking help and growth. My vision is for this organization to assist us in holding steady the guidelines of integrity and clear intent given to us by Enoch. England holds the heart of our planet, so I cannot think of a better place to locate the heart of Zimbaté.

Namaste,
Carolyn

ZIMBATÉ INTERNATIONAL

OUR MISSION STATEMENT

Zimbaté International has been established to protect the lineage of Zimbaté and preserve the sacred wisdom gifted and entrusted to us by Enoch.

Zimbaté International will ensure that the lineage remains true in its original form and intent.

Zimbaté International has been created to support its membership of practitioners and teachers and to assist each member in developing his or her own personal and professional paths while maintaining high standards of intent and integrity in their work.

BIOGRAPHY OF CAROLYN SNYDER

Carolyn became a Reiki Master in 1984. She is a teacher, lecturer, personal consultant, and NLP programmer. After several years of study, she wrote and developed a teaching protocol for Zimbaté--the first person within this age to do so. Zimbaté is a "new" old modality that, although in its infancy, is being well and widely received by students and clients alike. Carolyn has taught in the USA as well as in the UK. She has been teaching in the UK two to three times a year since 2006. The reception and results of her classes has shown the power and possibilities for Zimbaté. Her web site is zimbatehealing.com and she can contacted at carolyn@zimbatehealing.com

Printed in Great Britain
by Amazon